Favorite
Hungarian Recipes

Favorite Hungarian Recipes

BY

LILLA DEELEY

Illustrated by
L. FARKAS
and
Z. POHÁRNOK

DOVER PUBLICATIONS, INC.

NEW YORK

This Dover edition, first published in 1972, is an unabridged and unaltered republication of the work originally published by Hale, Cushman & Flint in 1938 under the title *Hungarian Cookery*.

International Standard Book Number: 0-486-22846-0
Library of Congress Catalog Card Number: 70-189343

Manufactured in the United States of America
Dover Publications, Inc.
180 Varick Street
New York, N.Y. 10014

INTRODUCTION

IF you have ever been to Hungary and feasted on the delicious food of that country you will welcome this little book. If you have never known such delights you now have the chance of enjoying some of them at home.

Hungarian cookery is considered by leading experts to rank next to French cuisine in importance. It is certainly one of the most characteristic among national cuisines. Many of the most famous Hungarian dishes and ingredients owe their origin to people and tribes which invaded Hungary from time to time ; but so strong are the racial qualities of the Hungarians that they assimilate strange food and strange customs so thoroughly that in a comparatively short time these become national features. To illustrate this suffice it to mention that paprika, the chief condiment of Hungarian national dishes, was introduced by the Turks in the sixteenth century.

Numerous Hungarian dishes were introduced by the different races which inhabited the country permanently or otherwise and mingled with the Hungarian population—Gipsies, Slavs, Saxons, Souabes. Spices and other ingredients have been added to traditional dishes by generations of Hungarian cooks and housewives. They have become the staple food and most patriots would indignantly deny that their favourite dishes are of foreign origin.

Hungarian dishes are tasty and rather highly spiced, but not nearly so " hot " as the curried dishes of India or some of the national dishes of Spain or Latin America. Spanish pimento and cayenne pepper are very sharp condiments and never used in Hungary. When buying paprika one should always insist on getting genuine Hungarian " rose-paprika " which is obtainable in all good-class stores. The best is produced at Szeged, in the south of Hungary. This paprika is very mild, and most paprika dishes are thickened by sour cream or tomato-pulp to mitigate any sharpness.

Green or red paprika pods, the fruits of the paprika plant (capsicum) are also used in different ways in Hungary. The round variety is generally sweeter in flavour than the long, pointed fruits. Paprika fruit, called shortly paprika in Hungarian, can be obtained nowadays almost everywhere all the year round, as they are cultivated in gardens and in hot-houses in most countries. They are also obtainable tinned but, except for salads, the fresh fruits are preferable for stews and other cooked dishes.

The recipes for Hungarian sweets and cakes deserve special attention for every cook in Hungary is an accomplished pastry-maker. The different home-made pastries play an important part in the daily menu— home-made noodles and other pastes accompany stews; others are boiled, sautée in hot lard, strewn with minced cabbage, minced ham, scrambled eggs, browned semolina, and so on, and served as savouries. Or strewn with grated nuts, poppy-seeds, jam, cream-cheese or other ingredients and served as sweets. Only a few examples are given in this book as there are many amongst them which would not appeal to all palates, but those given are well worth trying.

The dishes described here are calculated to suffice for six persons, and for rather liberal portions. When planning a meal consisting of more than three courses, the quantities given will be enough for eight persons. The recipes are simple and easy to follow. The ingredients and condiments are nowadays obtainable at every good-class food-store.

Hungary has always been considered the granary of Europe. The freshness and excellence of its food products has raised the art of cooking to a high level, and the delight in good cooking is shown by even the humblest Hungarian. It is to be hoped that this little book will help to introduce into English homes the many delicious Hungarian dishes and wines with which only the lucky few, who have travelled in Hungary, have hitherto been acquainted.

CONTENTS

CONVERSION TABLES FOR FOREIGN EQUIVALENTS

DRY INGREDIENTS

Ounces	Grams	Grams	Ounces	Pounds	Kilograms	Kilograms	Pounds
1 =	28.35	1 =	0.035	1 =	0.454	1 =	2.205
2	56.70	2	0.07	2	0.91	2	4.41
3	85.05	3	0.11	3	1.36	3	6.61
4	113.40	4	0.14	4	1.81	4	8.82
5	141.75	5	0.18	5	2.27	5	11.02
6	170.10	6	0.21	6	2.72	6	13.23
7	198.45	7	0.25	7	3.18	7	15.43
8	226.80	8	0.28	8	3.63	8	17.64
9	255.15	9	0.32	9	4.08	9	19.84
10	283.50	10	0.35	10	4.54	10	22.05
11	311.85	11	0.39	11	4.99	11	24.26
12	340.20	12	0.42	12	5.44	12	26.46
13	368.55	13	0.46	13	5.90	13	28.67
14	396.90	14	0.49	14	6.35	14	30.87
15	425.25	15	0.53	15	6.81	15	33.08
16	453.60	16	0.57				

LIQUID INGREDIENTS

Liquid Ounces	Milliliters	Milliliters	Liquid Ounces	Quarts	Liters	Liters	Quarts
1 =	29.573	1 =	0.034	1 =	0.946	1 =	1.057
2	59.15	2	0.07	2	1.89	2	2.11
3	88.72	3	0.10	3	2.84	3	3.17
4	118.30	4	0.14	4	3.79	4	4.23
5	147.87	5	0.17	5	4.73	5	5.28
6	177.44	6	0.20	6	5.68	6	6.34
7	207.02	7	0.24	7	6.62	7	7.40
8	236.59	8	0.27	8	7.57	8	8.45
9	266.16	9	0.30	9	8.52	9	9.51
10	295.73	10	0.33	10	9.47	10	10.57

Gallons (American)	Liters	Liters	Gallons (American)
1 =	3.785	1 =	0.264
2	7.57	2	0.53
3	11.36	3	0.79
4	15.14	4	1.06
5	18.93	5	1.32
6	22.71	6	1.59
7	26.50	7	1.85
8	30.28	8	2.11
9	34.07	9	2.38
10	37.86	10	2.74

HORS D'ŒUVRE

To serve cold hors d'œuvre is the exception rather than the rule in Hungary. The chief reason for this is the general habit of taking a snack-meal between breakfast and lunch, called "tizórai," meaning 10 o'clock meal. This consists of ham, or sausage rolls, or bread-and-dripping, or scrambled eggs, or warm sausages with mustard or horse-radish. Everybody having enjoyed such a snack-meal, cold hors d'œuvre is only served before very elaborate lunches or dinners. In general all sorts of salads, Hungarian sausages—such as the famous salami and kolbász—jellied ham and fish, etc., are served. Here follow a few Hungarian recipes for cold egg-dishes, suitable for hors d'œuvre.

BORSOS TOJAS
(*Peppered eggs*)

Six hard-boiled eggs are finely chopped, mixed with 1 oz. creamed butter, a little made mustard, salt, pepper and paprika. Press into suitable fancy mould, turn out, garnish with radishes and small new onions.

9

MUSTÁR TOJÁS
(*Mustard eggs*)

Shell and cut into halves 6 hard-boiled eggs ; remove yolk and cream with $1\frac{1}{2}$ oz. butter, 1 teaspoonful anchovy paste, a little made mustard, salad oil, lemon juice and finely chopped parsley and chive. Put this mixture into a forcing bag, fill into the scooped egg-whites, place them on ice, and garnish—before serving—with jelly and chopped ham.

TÖLTÖTT TOJÁS
(*Stuffed eggs*)

Similar method to ." mustard " eggs ; cream the hard-boiled yolks with finely minced sardines, butter, lemon juice ; decorate the dish with jelly, caviar and thin slices of smoked salmon.

SOUPS

SOUPS play an important part in the menus of Hungarian families.
The chief meal is eaten in the middle of the day, whenever possible, and
the midday dinner invariably begins with a soup. No effort or work is
spared to make the soup tasty and nourishing; consequently it is
quite often the chief course of the dinner, especially if it takes the
form of a broth, containing fish, fowl or meat. It is then usually followed
by a substantial savoury dish, of which examples will be given in this
book.

So strong is tradition amongst the Hungarians for a warm midday
meal that even farm and industrial workers insist on it; it is the usual
sight in the country to see the female members of the family carrying
the midday meal to the fields in a specially constructed, tiered carrier,
which also keeps the courses warm. The same applies to town workers;
the midday pause finds wives in long queues waiting outside factories.
However poor the people may be, there is sure to be a tasty meal for
the family; for work, effort and loving care in preparing the meals
are never stinted.

11

BÁRÁNY LEVES
(Lamb broth)

The head, liver and lung of a lamb should be slowly boiled in very little water, together with a piece of bacon, parsley, some sliced carrots, celery-root and salt. Meanwhile fry in 1 oz. butter, 1 oz. flour, stir in the strained soup, and add the head, liver, lung, bacon, and vegetables, all cut into small dice.

BARNA LEVES MÁJAS HALUSKÁVAL
(Brown soup with liver dumplings)

Prepare 2 pints good, brown, clear soup. Put through the mincing machine 4 oz. calf's liver and 3 or 4 slices stale bread (previously soaked in milk). Mix the chopped liver and bread with a little fried and chopped onion and parsley, 1 egg, season with salt, pepper and powdered marjoram; add a little flour, if it is too sloppy; it should be rather firm. Make tiny balls of the mixture, cook in the boiling soup for 10 minutes and serve.

BARNA LEVES MÁJRIZZSEL
(Brown soup with liver rice)

Prepare in exactly the same way as the above, but instead of shaping the mixture into small balls, press it through a coarsely meshed sieve straight into the boiling soup.

BURGONYA LEVES
(Potato soup)

Peel and cut into small dice 1 lb. potatoes. Fry in 1 oz. lard, 1 oz. flour, $\frac{1}{2}$ teaspoonful each of finely chopped onion and parsley, $\frac{1}{2}$ teaspoonful paprika; add slowly 1$\frac{1}{2}$ pints water, 1 or 2 pieces bone, and lastly the potatoes. Season with salt and boil, until the potatoes are tender. Stir 1 teaspoonful butter with 1 gill thick cream and mix with soup, just before serving. On meatless days chopped ham is added.

CSIRKE LEVES
(*Chicken broth*)

Cut up into neat joints 1 large fowl, fry in butter, together with chopped parsley, carrot, celery and leek ; season with salt and add enough warm water to just cover the meat. Boil slowly for 2 to 3 hours. Fry in 1 oz. butter, 1 oz. flour, add little by little 1½ pints of the strained soup and, just before serving, 1 gill of cream and a little lemon juice.

GOMBA LEVES
(*Mushroom soup*)

Clean and cut into thin slices 4 oz. mushrooms, place them into a small saucepan, together with 1 oz. butter and ½ teaspoonful each of finely chopped shallots and parsley. Stew slowly for 15 minutes. Meanwhile fry in 1 oz. butter, 1 oz. flour, add slowly 1½ pints white stock ; cook for 10 minutes, then add the stewed mushrooms, 1 gill thick cream and a squeeze of lemon. Season with salt and pepper just before serving.

GULYÁS LEVES
(*Hungarian broth*)

Warm an iron saucepan, then throw in 1 spoonful lard, 1 oz. fat bacon cut into small dice, 1 oz. chopped onion, ½ coffeespoonful paprika, ½ lb. beef cut into small dice, 1 teaspoonful vinegar ; season with salt, pepper and a little chopped cumin seeds, add slowly 1½ pints water. Stew under lid for 1½ hours, then add ½ lb. parboiled potatoes, cut into small pieces, continue boiling for another 15 minutes. Some boiled haricot beans and soup-noodles are usually added in Hungary, where this broth is served as the chief dish of the meal. Instead of beans, barley may be used.

HALLEVES
(*Fish soup*)

Grate finely 1 piece each of carrot, red onion, turnip, celery and potato ; place the mashed vegetables into a saucepan, together with a little water, lemon juice, season with pepper and salt, cook for 1 hour and press through fine sieve. Fry 1½ oz. lard, 1½ oz. flour, add slowly 1½ pints fish-stock (prepared by boiling the head and bones of the fish), then the vegetable mash, stirring all the time, in order to make a thick, smooth soup. Just before serving add small balls of fish forcemeat or small pieces of flaked, boiled fish.

HÚSLEVES ZSEMLYEGOMBÓCCAL
(*Clear soup with dumplings*)

Prepare 2 pints strong, clear soup in the usual way by boiling beef, bones, vegetables for at least 2 hours. Meanwhile cut into small dice 3 breakfast rolls, or 4 slices white bread ; dry these dice a little under the grill, but do not allow to brown. Fry them in ½ oz. lard, together with a little chopped parsley—again do not allow to brown. Mix with 2 eggs, a little milk and enough flour to make a firm dough ; season with salt, form into tiny balls and cook in the boiling, clear soup for 5 or 6 minutes.

KORHELY LEVES
(*Cabbage soup*)

This is a traditional dish, served in Hungary in the early hours of the morning, after a night of dancing, gambling or other gay activities, and is considered as a " pick-me-up " ; the famous onion soup of France serves a similar purpose. " Korhely " means " dissipated." The racy Hungarian language teems with these strong, exaggerated expressions. Boil for ¼ hour 1 lb. " Sauerkraut " (pickled cabbage). Meanwhile fry in 1½ oz. lard 2 oz. flour and 2 oz. chopped, red onion. Season liberally with paprika, add first the liquid part of the cabbage stew, then the roughly chopped cabbage, small pieces of smoked sausage (kolbász) and, just before serving, 1 gill sour cream.

14

MÁJ LEVES
(*Liver soup*)

Cook 5 oz. calf's liver, together with 1 onion and 1 carrot, until tender ; then strain the soup off, mince the liver, onion and carrot very finely through mincing machine. Fry 1 oz. butter, 1 oz. flour, add slowly the strained soup and lastly the minced liver and vegetables. Serve with croutons (small dice of white bread, fried in butter).

RÁKLEVES
(*Crayfish soup*)

Wash thoroughly about 20 pieces of small, living crayfish. Throw them into boiling, salted water, to which add a teaspoonful cumin seed, a sprig of dill, 1 chopped shallot, 1 leek, 1 carrot and ½ celery. Strain the soup and boil again very quickly to reduce. Meanwhile remove the meat from the claws and keep warm. Pound in a mortar the feet and bodies to a pulp, mix it with butter and a little soup ; stir this mixture into the reduced soup. Place the meat from the claws into a tureen, pour the soup over them and serve steaming hot.

RIZS LEVES
(*Rice soup*)

Clean, wash and dry thoroughly, 2 oz. rice, then fry lightly in 1 oz. butter, until the rice becomes transparent, but do not allow to brown. Mix a little finely chopped parsley and shallot to the rice, season with a little paprika and add 2 pints warm water. Boil for ½ hour and just before serving, stir in 1 gill thick cream and 1 egg-yolk.

15

SZEGEDI HALÁSZLÉ
(*Fish-broth*)

Szeged is the centre of the paprika production and this town is famous for its paprika cookery. This is the traditional soup of Hungarian fishermen.

Several kinds of fresh-water fish should be taken, such as carp, pike, etc. Clean the fish with a damp cloth (do not wash), rub with salt and cut into dice. Fry in 1 oz. lard 1 or 2 chopped onions, add 1 coffee-spoonful paprika and 1 pint water; boil therein all the fish-bones and heads for ½ hour; strain the soup, add the fish and boil for 20 minutes, shaking the pot from time to time, but without stirring.

ZÖLDBAB LEVES
(*Haricots verts-soup*)

Boil ½ lb. haricots-verts until tender. Fry in 1 oz. butter 1 oz. flour a little chopped onion and parsley, add the haricot soup and the finely cut beans. Season with salt, pepper, lemon juice and just before serving, add 1 gill thick cream and a little chopped dill or mint.

FISH

Hungary being an inland country, sea-fish are not popular. Salt-water fish only reaches Hungary in chilled or salted or smoked condition. Chilled salmon is used for elaborate meals and in the restaurants ; salted or smoked fish are in demand for Lenten dishes ; Lenten days are strictly kept even by people who are otherwise not practising Catholics. It is a tradition which has become a habit.

Sweetwater fish are to be had in great variety and are prepared in many delicious ways. Most typical are the stews.

Lake Balaton supplies a unique and world-famous fish—the " Fogas."

17

BOGRÁCSOS HAL
(*Fish stew*)

" Bogrács " is the name of the earthenware stew-pan, beloved by all Hungarian cooks, as it is supposed to give the best results in preparing stews. In country homes the stews are often served in the " Bogrács." Take several kinds of fish, such as carp, sturgeon, or other white sweet-water fish, scale and cut into large pieces ; place the fish with the fish-blood into the stew-pan, with enough water just to cover it, add salt and 1 or 2 sliced red onions. Boil quickly for 15 minutes, then add ½ tea-spoonful sweet Hungarian paprika and boil now in very moderately warm oven for a further 30 minutes. On no account should the fish be stirred, but shake the " bogrács " from time to time vigorously. Serve in the same dish.

HALPAPRIKÁS
(*Fish stew*)

This is the traditional dish of Hungarian fishermen. Only fresh-water fish are used, as many kinds as are available, such as sterlet, pike, carp, perch. Clean and scale the fish, wipe with a wet cloth but do not wash them. Then remove all bones, cut into neat pieces, place them in a jar, sprinkle with salt and let them stand for at least ½ hour. Meanwhile fry in 2 oz. lard 4 oz. sliced, red onions a nice golden colour, add ½ tea-spoonful sweet paprika and about 1 pint stock (prepared by cooking the fish-bones and heads). Drain now the pieces of fish, rub the salt off with a dry cloth and place them in the paprika sauce ; stew slowly for 15 minutes, shaking from time to time the stew-pan. Just before serving, thicken the sauce with 1 gill cream.

HALPÖRKÖLT
(*Fish stew*)

Same method as " Halpaprikás," but instead of thick cream, add, together with the fish, 2 to 3 spoonfuls tomato pulp.

KIRÁNTOTT HAL
(*Fried fish*)

Take for each person 2 fillets of river-fish, pull out carefully all the bones, dry with a clean cloth, roll in flour, beaten egg, fine dry breadcrumbs and fry the fillets in deep, boiling lard. Drain and serve with fresh, crisp lettuce salad.

KOCSONYÁZOTT HAL
(*Jellied fish*)

Trout ("pisztráng"), or sturgeon ("kecsege") may be used for this dish. Poach the fish in boiling water, to which add a little lemon juice, onion, coarse pepper and salt. When the fish is tender, take it out and reduce the soup by boiling quickly for $\frac{1}{2}$ hour, strain and add a few pieces gelatine. Pour some of the jelly in a suitable mould, decorate with fancy shapes of pickled beetroot and cooked carrots, dispose the pieces of fish and pour some of the jelly to cover. Continue until all is used. Serve very cold.

PONTY VAJBAN
(*Carp in butter*)

Clean, scale and wipe with a wet cloth a carp, weighing about 3 to 4 lbs. Make a few incisions on the edges and sprinkle with salt. Line the bottom of an oval, fireproof dish—previously brushed with melted butter—with sliced, parboiled potatoes, place the fish on top of potatoes, pour 2 gills fresh cream over and 6 oz. butter, cut into small pieces. Bake in oven, basting frequently. Serve in the same dish.

RÁC PONTY
(*Serbian carp*)

This dish, of Serbian origin, is very popular in the south of Hungary. One large carp, weighing about 3 lbs., is scaled, cleaned and rubbed with salt outside and inside. Cover the bottom of a baking pan with sliced, parboiled potatoes, place the fish on top and scatter over fish and potatoes small pieces of butter, about 3 oz. altogether. Bake in a warm oven for 15-20 minutes. Meanwhile mix in a cup 2 gills milk or cream with a teaspoonful Hungarian paprika, and pour this mixture over the fish, replace and bake for another ¼ hour. Another portion of cream and paprika should be added for the last 5 minutes in the oven. Serve either in the fish-pan in which cooked, or lift over carefully potatoes and fish on to a warm dish, pour the creamed gravy over and serve very warm. In some places the fish is covered with sliced tomatoes and thinly sliced green paprika fruit, before baking the fish.

SZEGEDI HARCSÁS KÁPOSZTA
(Fishpie of Szeged)

" Harcsa " is a kind of white shad, but its flesh is finer ; it is caught in the Danube and the Tisza, the two main rivers of Hungary. One of the many ways in which the famous cooks of the town Szeged prepare this popular fish is this : scale, clean and cut the fish into neat pieces, remove all bones, sprinkle with salt. Fry in 1 oz. lard 1 oz. flour and 1 or 2 sliced, red onions, ½ teaspoonful paprika, add 1½ lbs. pickled cabbage (" savanyú káposzta ") and cook for 1 hour. Drain the fish (the salt draws out the water), add to the cabbage and cook slowly for 20 minutes, shaking the pan from time to time. Any river fish may be used and cooked in this way.

ENTRÉES

THE following dishes are suitable as chief dish for lunch or supper, or to serve before the meat course at dinner.

GOMBÁS MÁJ
(*Mushroom and liver*)

Clean and dry ½ lb. of fine, large mushrooms, brown carefully in butter, season with salt, pepper and chopped parsley. Keep warm. Meanwhile dust with flour 6 thin slices of calf's liver, fry quickly on both sides in butter or lard, place on warm platter, pile the fried mushroom on top of the fried slices of liver, garnish with fried potatoes and serve with a good gravy.

GOMBÁS HÚS
(*Mushroom and beef*)

Clean, dry and chop roughly ½ lb. of mushrooms, fry—together with
1 oz. chopped red onion—in lard, season with salt and freshly ground
pepper. Spread this mixture on 6 large, thin slices of beef, roll tightly
each fillet, tie with cotton, and place the rolls into a saucepan, fry them
quickly in lard, add enough stock to just cover, and stew under lid for
1½ hours, basting frequently and replacing the stock as it boils away.
Serve with potato cakes.

GOMBÁS RIZS
(*Mushroom and rice*)

Clean ½ lb. rice, stew in saucepan together with 3 oz. lard; when the
rice becomes glassy (do not allow to brown) add enough water to cover.
Meanwhile fry and stew 6 oz. roughly chopped mushrooms, also boil
3 oz. green peas until tender. When all is cooked, mix rice, mushrooms
and peas, pile high on a hot dish, sprinkle with grated cheese and serve
at once.

LECSÓ
(*Scrambled eggs with pepperfruit*)

Cut up a large paprika fruit (pimento) crosswise into thin strips, after
scraping out the seeds. Slice thinly 2 young onions, cut up 5 or 6 ripe
tomatoes. Stew all gently with a little lard, under cover, for 15 minutes.
Add now 6 well-beaten eggs, stirring all the time, and cook until the
eggs are set. Season with salt and paprika. (N.B.—If fresh paprika
fruit or tomatoes not available, tinned may be used.)

MÁJ PÖRKÖLT
(*Hungarian liver stew*)

Cut 1 lb. calf's liver into dice, about 1½ in. in diameter, fry together with
3 oz. sliced onions in 2 oz. lard, stirring all the time. Add a little brown
gravy and stew slowly for ½ hour; thicken the gravy with sour cream
and season the stew, just before serving, with salt, pepper and paprika.
Serve with mashed potatoes.

RAKOTT VARGÁNYA
(*Mushroom pie*)

Brush a fireproof dish with melted butter, place into it neatly 1 lb. fresh, large mushrooms ; sprinkle each layer with salt, finely chopped parsley, grated cheese and melted butter. Place into moderate oven and baste rather frequently, with a few spoonfuls at a time, of thick cream.

RAKOTT BURGONYA (1)
(*Potato pie*)

There are several Hungarian recipes for this dish. Here follow the most popular varieties :

Ten to twelve King Edward potatoes should be cooked in their jackets, then peeled, mashed and mixed with 2 oz. butter, 3 eggs, 2 gills milk or cream, salt and pepper, 5 oz. chopped, smoked sausage. Brush a fireproof dish with melted butter, sprinkle with fine breadcrumbs and fold in half of the potato mixture ; place on it a layer of sliced hard-boiled eggs (3 eggs) and finish with the rest of the potatoes. Sprinkle top with grated cheese, breadcrumbs and a few spoonfuls of melted butter. Place in a warm oven for 20 minutes.

RAKOTT BURGONYA (2)
(*Potato pie*)

Boil 1 lb. of yellow, Dutch potatoes in their jackets, peel thinly and cut them into slices ; cut 3 hard-boiled eggs into similar slices ; chop 3 oz. boiled ham roughly. Brush a fireproof dish with melted butter, dust with fine breadcrumbs, place into the dish layerwise potatoes, eggs and ham, seasoning each layer with salt and pepper. Beat a raw egg-yolk with 1 gill thick sour cream, pour into the dish, sprinkle top with breadcrumbs and melted butter. Bake in moderate oven for 20 minutes. This is a Lenten dish, and is usually served on " fasting " days as the chief course for lunch or dinner.

RAKOTT BURGONYA (3)
(Potatoe pie)

Same procedure as Potato Pie No. 2, but instead of boiled ham, use slices of some highly spiced, smoked, skinned sausage. In Hungary the popular sausage called " Kolbász " is used, but it may be substituted by any good, smoked sausage, according to taste. If sausage is used, the pie, of course, must not be served as a Lenten dish, and instead of butter, lard may be used.

TÖLTÖTT PAPRIKA
(Stuffed green peppers)

Take for each person 1 green pepper, cut away the stalk, scrape out the seeds, pour boiling water over them and let them stand in the water for 10 to 15 minutes. Meanwhile prepare the stuffing. For 6 persons, i.e. to stuff 6 green peppers, melt 1 oz. lard, stir in 2 oz. rice, add a little white stock and boil until the rice is tender. Brown in some dripping a teaspoonful each of finely chopped onions and parsley, blend with the cooked rice 1 egg and ½ lb. finely minced lean pork. Season the stuffing with salt and pepper and fill the peppers loosely with it. Take care to dry the peppers carefully before stuffing them. Prepare a thin, well-seasoned tomato sauce, place the stuffed peppers in it and let them boil for 1 hour. The peppers should be standing upright in the saucepan, or the filling will fall out. Serve with mashed potatoes.

TÖLTÖTT KÁPOSZTA
(Stuffed cabbage)

Take for each person 1 large, unbroken cabbage leaf, pour boiling salted water over them ; let them stand in the water for 15 minutes, then drain and place in the middle of each leaf a large spoonful of stuffing (same stuffing as for green peppers) ; roll the cabbage leaves round the stuffing, wrap round each roll a slice of fat bacon, tie with cotton or use small skewers. Melt a spoonful of lard in a suitable casserole or saucepan, place in it layerwise chopped onion and chopped fat bacon, then the cabbage rolls and cover them with good brown gravy. Stew for at least 1 hour, thicken the gravy with a few spoonfuls of thick, sour cream. Serve with mashed potatoes.

TOKÁNY
(*Lobscowes*)

" Tokány " may be prepared of lamb (" bárány-tokány "), veal (" borjú-tokány ") or pork (" disznó-tokány "). Cut up 1 lb. meat into small strips, season liberally with salt and paprika and fry, together with 1 or 2 sliced onions, in butter or lard. Add a little warm gravy and tomato pulp, and stew under lid for at least 1 hour or until tender. Thicken the gravy with a spoonful of cream just before serving.

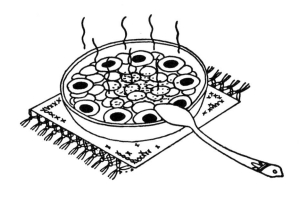

VELÖ TOJÁSSAL
(*Scrambled eggs and brain*)

Poach for a minute 2 or 3 calves' brains, skin and chop, fry in 3 oz. lard, together with ½ oz. of finely chopped shallots. Add, when almost ready, 6 well-beaten eggs ; finish, stirring all the time, and season with salt and paprika. It is ready as soon as the eggs are set. Sprinkle with chopped parsley and chive.

VESE GOMBÁVAL
(*Kidney and mushrooms*)

Clean thoroughly 1 large calf's kidney, cut into very thin slices. Melt in stewpan 1½ oz. lard, fry therein 1 oz. finely chopped onion, the sliced kidney and 5 oz. cleaned, sliced mushrooms. When all is fried, sprinkle in 1 teaspoonful flour, a little salt and paprika, mix thoroughly and add 1 gill thick cream to thicken.

VESE VELÖVEL
(*Kidney with brain*)

Cut into slices 1 well-cleaned calf's kidney. Poach for a minute 2 calves' brains, skin and chop roughly. Fry in 3 oz. butter 3 oz. chopped onions, together with the kidney and brain, stirring all the time. It takes about 15 to 20 minutes to prepare this delicious dish, which is seasoned with salt, pepper and marjoram.

STEWS

Stews play a large rôle in Hungarian cookery. It is the staple food of the people, and native cooks use all their ingenuity to concoct most appetising dishes of the cheapest cuts of meat, and even of scraps, with the help of dripping, onions and the national condiment—paprika. To thicken the gravy, tomato pulp or thick, sour cream is used, which also counteracts the sharpness of paprika. This latter is simply cream allowed to go sour.

BÁRÁNY PÖRKÖLT
(*Lamb stew*)

Fry in 1 oz. lard 2 oz. chopped, fresh bacon, 10 oz. sliced red onion, season with paprika, add 1 teaspoonful vinegar, 2 lbs. lamb, previously cut into large dice ; stir until the meat and onions are golden brown, then season with salt, add enough stock or water to cover and stew slowly for about 1 hour. Thicken the gravy with 1 gill tomato pulp. Just before serving, melt in a small frying pan ½ oz. butter, stir in quickly ½ teaspoonful of Hungarian paprika, add immediately a little warm water. Pour this liquid over the stew ; this gives the dish the coveted red colour, and the peculiar Hungarian flavour. This last-minute treatment should be remembered, whenever preparing a Hungarian stew. In exactly the same way are prepared *Birka*-(mutton), *Disznó*-(pork), *Borjú*-(veal) *Pörkölt*.

BÁRÁNY PAPRIKÁS
(*Lamb stew*)

To be prepared in exactly the same way as " Pörkölt," but use as a thickening, instead of tomato pulp, 1 gill of thick, sour cream.
May be also prepared of mutton, veal, or pork.

BOGRÁCSOS CSIRKE
(*Casserole chicken*)

Cut up into neat joints 2 young chickens, sprinkle with salt. Heat in an earthenware or enamelled casserole 2 oz. lard, and fry therein 1 oz. finely chopped red onions, a puddingspoonful sweet Hungarian paprika, all the cut-up chicken-joints, stirring all the time. As soon as the chicken is fried, add 4 oz. sliced, cleaned mushrooms, 2 large spoonfuls tomato pulp and 1 or 2 gills of stock or water. Cover and stew in moderate oven for 1½ hours. Add parboiled, skinned, small new potatoes and stew for another ½ hour or until all the ingredients are tender. Shake the casserole from time to time to prevent sticking. A few minutes before serving stir 1 gill sour cream into the gravy. If possible, serve in the same dish. Sprinkle top with chopped parsley.

CIGÁNY GULYÁS

(*Gipsy stew*)

Gipsy stew is very tasty and may be prepared of any odd pieces of meat, such as beef, veal, pork, mutton, oxtail, heart, tripe, sweetbread, etc., altogether 2½ to 3 lbs. Cut everything into uniform, neat dice, sprinkle liberally with salt, pepper and paprika. Warm thoroughly a suitable earthenware or copper stewing pan ; throw in first a few slices roughly chopped, fresh, fat bacon ; when it begins to melt, add 3 or 4 pieces chopped red onions ; add the pieces of meat, a few pieces of sweet corn (kukorica), enough water to cover, and stew slowly for 3 hours. Add more water from time to time. Shortly before serving, add boiled, quartered potatoes. Serve in the same dish in which the stew was cooked.

KOLOZSVÁRI KÁPOSZTA

(*Transsylvanian pork and cabbage pie*)

This dish is of Saxon origin ; Saxons have lived in closed settlements since the Middle Ages in Transsylvania. Kolozsvár (or Klausenburg) is the old capital of this ancient and beautiful country, now belonging to Roumania.

Take 2 lbs. sauerkraut (pickled white cabbage), place it into a saucepan, together with 2-3 tablespoonfuls of dripping and stew for 1 hour. Meanwhile cut into neat dice 2 lbs. lean pork, chop roughly 4 pieces red onions, stir into 1 oz. melted lard, season liberally with sweet Hungarian paprika (red pepper) and salt. When meat and onions are nicely browned, add enough white stock to cover and stew for 1 hour. Cook 3 oz. rice with ½ onion until soft. Line the bottom of an earthenware dish, which should be fireproof, with thin slices of bacon, place layerwise cabbage, pork and rice, until all is used, taking care that the top layer is cabbage. Season each layer with freshly ground pepper. Stir ½ teaspoonful paprika into ½ pint cream, pour this into the dish, place into moderate oven for ½ hour. Serve in the same dish.

LUCSKOS KÁPOSZTA
(*Transsylvanian-Saxon stew*)

The title means " sloppy cabbage." Select 1 or 2 small, very firm, white cabbages, cut each into 4 to 6 wedge-shaped pieces, throw them into boiling, salted water and cook for ½ hour. Cook separately 1 lb. lean pork and ½ lb. beef. Drain the cabbage, press out all water and place the wedge-shaped pieces into a fireproof earthenware pot ; cut the boiled beef and pork into suitable pieces, mix with the cabbage, season with salt and pepper, add a bouquet of dill, marjoram and parsley, enough soup to cover and a little vinegar. Before serving, mix in a few spoonfuls of thick, sour cream. Mashed potatoes accompany this dish.

MAGYAR GULYÁS
(*Hungarian stew*)

This famous dish is seldom prepared in the correct way outside Hungary, although quite easy to cook, if the directions are closely followed.
Take 2 lbs. boneless, very lean beef, cut into neat, large dice, about 2 to 2½ in. thick. Warm first thoroughly the earthenware, copper or iron stewpan, melt therein 2 oz. lard, fry 2 large, red onions (previously cut into fine slices), but do not allow to brown. Add now the meat (previously washed, but not dried), shake the pan and stir, until meat and onions are a golden brown colour ; season with salt and paprika, add a little tomato pulp, a few cumin seeds and just enough warm stock to cover. Put on the lid and stew very slowly for 2 to 3 hours, adding stock as it boils away. When the meat is quite soft, add boiled, quartered potatoes and cook for another 10 minutes, mixing potatoes and meat thoroughly. Add colour, as explained in recipe for " pörkölt."

SZEGEDI GULYÁS
(*Szeged stew*)

The town Szeged is famous for its cuisine ; being the centre of the paprika industry, the dishes of this southern town are very spicy. The stew is prepared of beef, in the same way, as Hungarian gulyás, but instead of lard, dice of fresh bacon are used for frying meat and onions. Instead of adding stock, 2 lbs. " savanyukáposzta " (sauerkraut, i.e.

pickled white cabbage) are added and only very little water. Shake the stewpan from time to time to prevent burning, but avoid stirring. Just before serving, pour in 1 gill thick, sour cream and colour, as described in recipe for " pörkölt."

SZÉKELY GULYÁS
(*Transsylvanian stew*)
Same as Szeged stew, but instead of beef, take pork.

TÖKPAPRIKÁS
(*Paprika-meat with vegetable marrow*)
Peel one tender young vegetable marrow, scrape out the seeds and cut the marrow into neat dice ; place in an earthenware bowl, sprinkle with a handful of salt. Cut into similar pieces 2 lbs. boneless meat (veal, pork or beef). Melt in an enamelled or earthenware stewpan 2 oz. lard, fry therein 4 oz. grated red onions and a tablespoonful Hungarian sweet paprika ; add the meat (previously washed in cold water) and fry until all pieces are a golden colour. Add 2 tablespoonful tomato pulp, cover and stew slowly for 1 hour. Add now the diced vegetable marrow, mix well with meat, cover and stew for another hour. When meat and marrow are tender, stir in 2 gills sour cream, sprinkle with finely chopped dill or other aromatic herb (sage or mint) and serve either in the casserole or in a covered dish. Serve with new potatoes.

31

ROASTS. STEAKS

ONLY the recipes of such steaks and roasts are given below which differ from those of other countries. They should provide a welcome variety from plain steaks and roasts.

BORJÚSZELET VADÁSZMÓDRA
(Hunters' veal steaks)

Take 6 nice slices of veal steaks, sprinkle with salt and pepper, brown them in a casserole with a spoonful butter; as soon as they change colour, sprinkle with a spoonful flour, add 2 oz. chopped, cooked ham, one glassful each of stock and white wine and a little chopped parsley. Stew for ½ hour, then lift out meat and keep warm. Reduce the gravy by boiling it for a few minutes quickly, season with a squeeze of lemon and thicken with a small piece of butter, rolled in flour. Pour over the steaks just before serving.

ESZTERHÁZY ROSTÉLYOS
(Beefsteak à la Eszterházy)

This is one of the most famous Hungarian dishes, named after the leading noble family, the greatest landowners in Hungary.
Take a very nice piece of round beef steak, weighing about 3 to 4 lbs., boneless. Grill in the oven in the usual way for 15 minutes. Meanwhile cut into thin strips (Julienne) ½ celery, 1 large carrot, 2 oz. onion and stew these vegetables for a few minutes with 1 oz. butter. Place now the steak into a stewpan, add the vegetables, drippings from steak, paprika, salt, pepper, and from time to time, baste the steak with thick cream. Before serving, cut the steak into thin slices, garnish with the stewed Julienne of vegetables and potatoes.

HONVÉD SZELET
(Soldiers' steaks)

" Honvéd " is the name for soldiers of the national army.
Cut into rather thick slices 2 lbs. boneless veal; lard liberally with thin strips of fat, uncured bacon. Melt in a stewpan 1½ oz. lard, fry therein 1½ oz. sliced red onion, add ½ teaspoonful paprika, the larded veal steaks, turning them in the hot, melted lard until they are a golden brown colour. Then add a little stock and stew for a few minutes. Pile high on a dish, pour the gravy over the steaks and surround with potatoes.

KOLBÁSZOS HÚS
(Pork stuffed with sausage)

Remove the bones from a shoulder of pork, taking care not to make holes into the meat. In place of the bones, put some skinned, smoked highly spiced sausages (in Hungary " kolbász " is used). Roll the meat and secure with skewer or cotton, score the skin in narrow strips or dice. Rub with salt and a piece of garlic, place into very hot oven, basting frequently with stock. Allow ½ hour to each lb. of meat. Serve with fried potatoes and pickled beetroots. The sausage stuffing gives it a peculiar taste.

PESTI VESEPECSENYE
(Roast beef of Budapest)

Pest is the old-fashioned name of the capital of Hungary.
Cut into small strips 2 oz. fat, uncured bacon, lard with these 2½ lbs. rump of beef, rub with salt and pepper and roast for 10 minutes in a hot oven, basting frequently. Meanwhile fry in 2 oz. lard 2 oz. chopped bacon and 3 oz. chopped onion ; add a little paprika and vinegar, sprinkle in 1 oz. flour ; place the meat now in a large copper or iron pan, pour over it the content of the frying pan, add a little stock and tomato pulp and braise for 1½ hours. Thicken the gravy with sour cream. Serve with " Galuska " (see recipe under " garnish ").

RABLÓHÚS, OR RABLÓPECSENYE
(Highwayman's mixed grill)

Take for 6 persons, 7 oz. each fillets of veal, beef and pork, 2 large red onions, 4 oz. sliced, fat bacon. The best meat for the purpose is under-cut, which should be cut in 1-in. thick, small, round steaks. Dust the steaks with salt, pepper and paprika, cut the onions into thin slices. Take for each person a skewer, about 5 to 6 in. long and place on them the ingredients in this order : a slice each of bacon, beef, onion ; bacon veal, onion ; bacon, pork, onion, bacon. When all six skewers are prepared in this way, they are grilled before an open fire, turning them round all the time and catching the gravy on sliced bread (which may

34

be placed on grid-iron). If an open fire is not available, the prepared skewers are first quickly fried in butter or lard, and then stewed for 15 minutes under cover. The gravy may be thickened with tomato pulp and cream, and the skewers served on a bed of cooked rice.

RAKOTT VESEPECSENYE

(*Hungarian hot-pot*)

Trim and brush with melted butter $2\frac{1}{2}$ lbs. boneless rumpsteak, grill for 10 minutes in hot oven, then cut into thin slices. Take a large fireproof dish, brush with melted dripping from meat, place layerwise sliced potatoes and meat, seasoning each layer with salt and pepper and moistening with thick cream. On each layer of meat, place a tea-spoonful of very finely chopped red onion. Cover and bake in oven until the potatoes are tender, which takes at least 1 hour. Baste from time to time with cream.

SZALONNÁS SÜLT
(*Larded Steak*)

Two to 2½ lbs. boneless round steak should be well trimmed and larded with small strips of fat bacon, previously rolled in paprika ; further, cover the steak with thin, large slices of bacon and secure with cotton. Place the meat into an iron pot, which should be just large enough to hold the meat, place it into hot oven, cover the casserole and roast for 1½ to 2 hours, adding just enough stock to prevent from burning. Just before serving, cut the meat into thin slices, pour over the gravy and garnish with potatoes and parsley.

SZOMBATHELYI SÜLT
(*Braised, stuffed beef rolls*)

Szombathely is the name of a town in West Hungary.
Flatten 6 large fillets of beef. Mix 2 oz. raw rice with 1 oz. chopped bacon, ½ oz. chopped onion, salt and pepper. Place a spoonful of this stuffing on each fillet, roll them and secure with skewers. Fry in a casserole 1½ oz. lard and 1 oz. chopped onion, place the rolls in the pan, fry quickly, add a little stock, cover and braise in oven for 1½ hours.

POULTRY

ROAST birds are usually prepared in Hungary as in any other country, but are almost always stuffed with a good, spiced bread stuffing and served with fresh lettuce salad and often with stewed fruit. Recipes for roast and boiled poultry are to be found in every cookery book. Only the Hungarian ways with stewed and braised poultry are given on the following pages.

CSÁSZÁR JÉRCE
(*Emperor's pullet*)

Fattened pullets are a speciality of the country and are exported to England in large numbers. Cut into neat joints a pullet weighing about 4 to 5 lbs., sprinkle with salt and place into casserole. Pour ¼ lb. boiling hot lard over the chicken, place into warm oven and roast for a few minutes until golden brown, basting frequently. Then add 2 spoonfuls at a time, thick, sweet cream, mixed with a little white wine. Altogether about 1 gill cream, and the same quantity wine should be used. 40-45 minutes should be sufficient to braise the chicken; when tender, lift out and keep warm. To the gravy add 2 spoonfuls each of cream, wine and stock, reduce by boiling quickly and serve in sauce-boat. Arrange the chicken nicely on a hot dish, garnish with fried potatoes, and serve with stewed or preserved fruits (cherries, pears, apples and prunes).

CSIRKE PAPRIKÁS
(*Paprika chicken*)

Quarter and sprinkle with salt 3 spring chickens, wash, clean and leave them in water until needed. Warm thoroughly a thick stewpan (copper or iron), melt 2 oz. lard, mix in 3 to 4 oz. chopped, red onions, do not allow to brown; stir in ½ teaspoonful paprika and 1 teaspoonful vinegar. Drain, but do not dry, the pieces of chicken, add to the contents of the stewing pan, shaking it to prevent burning. As soon as the chickens are lightly fried, but not brown, add a little stock, cover and stew for 40 to 45 minutes. Then add 3 spoonfuls thick, sour cream and small, boiled potatoes. Serve with " Galuska " or " Tarhonya." (See " Garnish.")

CSIRKE PÖRKÖLT

Same method of cooking as " paprikás," but instead of thickening the gravy with cream, use 2-3 spoonfuls tomato pulp. Same garnish.

PULYKA PÖRKÖLT
(*Turkey stew*)

Same method as chicken pörkölt, but should be stewed for at least 1½ hours, then coloured, like described in recipe for lamb stew.

RÁNTOTT CSIRKE
(*Fried chicken*)

Cut into neat joints 3 spring chickens, using only the best parts (the leaner parts may be used for " pörkölt "). Sprinkle lightly with salt, coat carefully and evenly first with flour, then dip in beaten egg and lastly coat with very fine, sieved dry breadcrumbs. Bring to boiling point 1 lb. refined lard; this should be done in a deep saucepan, so that the pieces of chicken may float in the fat. Do not fry too many pieces at the same time. When golden brown, lift out with straining spoon, place for a minute on sieve or blotting paper and keep warm, until all are done. Arrange on hot dish, garnish with parsley, fried potatoes and serve with it fresh, crisp lettuce salad. Warm tomato sauce is sometimes served with this dish, but is not usual.

VAGDALT LIBAMELLE
(*Minced goosebreast*)

Cut off the raw meat from the breast of a large goose, mince it very finely together with the goose liver, a spoonful finely minced, fried onion, 2 to 3 slices bread (previously soaked in milk); mix thoroughly, season with salt and pepper and add enough flour to hold together. Form into loaf, place on greased baking sheet or pan, baste with melted goose fat and roast for 45 minutes. Cut into slices and serve with the thickened gravy. This dish is sometimes eaten cold; in that case, it is baked covered with pastry, similarly to an English pork-pie. It is a suitable dish for cold buffet or picnic.

39

GAME

GAME is prepared in the well-known ways by the Hungarian cook. Following are a few exceptions.

FÜRJ SZÉKELY MÓDRA
(*Transsylvanian quail*)

Line with thin slices of fat bacon a suitable stew-pan, place in it layerwise pickled cabbage (sauerkraut), slices of streaky bacon, smoked sausage ("kolbász"), peeled and cored sour apples. Place on this three halved, flattened quails. Season each layer with salt, pepper and cumin seeds. Repeat layers, closing with cabbage. Pour ½ pint white wine into the dish, bake—without cover—in oven, basting frequently with its own juice. If possible, serve in same dish. The recipe is of Saxon origin.

NYÚLPÖRKÖLT. NYULPAPRIKÁS
(*Stewed hare*)

Same method as described for stewed veal, etc.

VADDISZNÓ PÖRKÖLT. VADDISZNÓ PAPRIKÁS
(*Stewed boar*)

Same method as stewed pork, etc. Same garnish.

SAUCES

ÁFONYA MÁRTÁS
(Cranberry sauce)

CLEAN ½ lb. cranberries, cook for a few minutes with very little water, a small glassful sweet white wine, the grated rind of ½ lemon, 1 orange, and the juice of the ½ lemon and 1 orange. Add sugar and spices according to taste. To serve with ducks, game and wild birds.

ECETES TORMAMÁRTÁS
(Cold horse radish sauce)

Grate finely a piece of strong horse radish, add a little white stock, sugar and vinegar. Serve with boiled beef or pork.

EGRES MÁRTÁS
(Gooseberry sauce)

One lb. of stewed gooseberries are pressed through a fine wire sieve. Fry in 1½ oz. butter 1½ oz. flour, add the gooseberry pulp and cook until a smooth sauce is obtained. Flavour with a little lemon juice and add sugar to taste. To serve with boiled beef or veal.

METÉLÖHAGYMA MÁRTÁS HIDEGEN
(Cold chive sauce)

Press through fine wire sieve the yolks of 3 hard-boiled eggs, mix with 3 spoonfuls salad oil, 1 spoonful vinegar, 2 spoonfuls finely chopped chives, season with salt and pepper. To serve with fish.

METÉLÖHAGYMA MÁRTÁS MELEGEN
(Warm chive sauce)

Fry in 1 oz. flour 2 spoonfuls finely chopped chives and 1 spoonful flour, stirring until light brown colour is obtained; then add a little water, 1 spoonful vinegar, 3 spoonfuls cream, salt, pepper. To serve with boiled meat.

PARADICSOM MÁRTÁS
(Tomato sauce)

Stew in 2 oz. lard 2 lbs. ripe tomatoes, together with ½ oz. each of chopped parsley and onion and very little water. Cook until a thick pulp is obtained; then pass through wire sieve. Meanwhile fry in 1 oz. butter 1 oz. flour, add a little stock and the tomato pulp. Season with salt and pepper and cook for at least 15 minutes. Then flavour with lemon juice, sugar and a spoonful of red wine. To serve with boiled or fried meat and poultry.

PAPRIKA MÁRTÁS
(*Paprika sauce*)

Fry in 2 oz. lard 4 oz. chopped red onion and 2 oz. flour, add ½ tea-spoonful paprika, 1 puddingspoonful vinegar, salt and little by little ½ pint warm stock or water. Cook for 15 minutes, thicken either with a few spoonfuls tomato pulp, or a small cupful thick cream. To be served with boiled fish, meat or poultry, also boiled sausages. Sausages and potatoes boiled in this sauce are a favourite snack in Hungary.

SALADS

GYÜMÖLCS SALÁTA
(*Fruit salad*)

Fruit salads are served in Hungary with almost all roast meats, poultry or game. Apricots, peaches, cherries, greengages, apples, pears, etc., may be served mixed or separately, according to taste. The fruits are carefully poached in a little water, with sugar and other flavouring, like lemon, almond, fruit-kernels, and, whenever possible, served chilled.

MAGYAR SALÁTA
(Hungarian salad)

Cut into thin slices ½ lb. boiled potatoes, ½ lb. large firm tomatoes and 3 large green pepper fruits. Arrange in separate groups in salad bowl or on dish, sprinkle with dressing (3 spoonfuls oil, 2 spoonfuls vinegar, salt, pepper and paprika). The red-white-green colour of the tomatoes, potatoes and peppers represent the national colours of Hungary.

VEGYES SALÁTA
(Mixed salad)

Boil separately ½ lb. potatoes, 1 large celery, 2 to 3 young onions and 1 piece of cauliflower. When ready, drain the different vegetables, cut potatoes and onions in slices, divide the cauliflower into small pieces, arrange in salad bowl on clean lettuce leaves, sprinkle with salad dressing of vinegar, oil, salt, pepper and mustard; decorate with sliced hard-boiled eggs.

ZÖLDPAPRIKA KÁPOSZTÁVAL TÖLTVE
(Pickled green pepper stuffed with cabbage)

Cut into fine shreds 2 white cabbages, sprinkle with salt. Clean 10 to 12 large green pepper fruits (fresh paprika fruit), cut out stem, scrape out seeds. Mix the shredded cabbage with cumin seeds, stuff it loosely into the peppers, place them into large, wide-necked glasses. Two pints vinegar, ½ pint water, shredded horse radish, mustard seeds, coarse pepper should be well mixed, boiled for a few minutes, and poured over the peppers. After a few days it is ready to eat. They may be served whole, or cut across into ½-in. thick slices.

VEGETABLES

PAPRIKÁS BURGONYA
(Paprika potatoes)

PREPARE a sauce as described under " Paprika Sauce," stew in it
$1\frac{1}{2}$ lb. firm, yellow potatoes, previously peeled and quartered. This is
excellent when served with boiled sausages (Frankfurt type).

RÁNTOTT KARFIOL
(Fried cauliflower)

Three small cauliflowers, boiled and drained, are coated with fine bread-crumbs and fried in deep, boiling lard until golden brown. Place them in a buttered fireproof dish, pour ½ pint fresh cream over them and place into moderately warm oven for a few minutes. Serve in same dish.

RÁNTOTT SPÁRGA
(Fried asparagus)

One and a half lbs. thick asparagus, boiled and drained, are cut into 2-in. long pieces, coated with flour, egg and fine breadcrumbs and fried golden yellow in deep, boiling lard. May be served as vegetable " entremets," between meat and sweet.

SPENÓT (OR PARAJ)
(Spinach)

Boil 2 lbs. spinach for 15 minutes and mince very finely. Fry in 1½ oz. butter 1½ oz. flour, a little chopped onion and parsley, add first a little stock, then the minced spinach, season with salt and pepper, cook for 10 minutes, then add 1 gill thick, sour cream and serve.

TEJFELES ÚJBURGONYA
(Creamed new potatoes)

Boil 2 lbs. new potatoes in their jackets until tender, skin carefully and sautée in butter for a few minutes. Cream 2 oz. butter, mix with 1 egg-yolk and 1 gill cream. Pour this mixture over the potatoes, gently heat, stirring all the time. Sprinkle with chopped parsley just before serving.

TÖKFŐZELÉK
(Creamed marrow)

Peel 1 large vegetable marrow, cut across and scrape out seeds. Then cut into neat cubes or strips, sprinkle liberally with salt and let it stand for 1 hour. Meanwhile fry in 1½ oz. butter 1½ oz. flour, a little parsley and onion (finely chopped), add milk (about 1½ gills) and cook, stirring all the time, until a very thick sauce is obtained. Press out all water from the marrow, add to the sauce and boil gently for ½ hour. Add ½ gill thick cream, a little lemon juice, paprika, and sprinkle the marrow a few minutes before serving with 1 spoonful finely chopped dill (or mint).

ZÖLDBAB FÖZELÉK
(Haricots verts or French beans)

Boil, without the lid on, 1½ lb. French beans, in salted water. When tender, cut slantwise into strips. Prepare a sauce as described under "vegetable marrow," cook the beans for 10 minutes in the cream-sauce, thicken with sour cream, season and serve.

ZÖLDPAPRIKA PARADICSOMMAL
(Green pepper stewed with tomatoes)

Clean 2 or 3 green pepper-fruits (fresh paprika fruit), scrape out seeds and cut across into thin strips. Peel and cut into thin slices 3 large, firm tomatoes, also ½ onion. Fry first the onion, then pepper in 1 oz. lard, then add tomatoes, cover and stew gently for 15 minutes; season with salt and pepper. This dish is served with omelettes, fish and meat.

GARNISH

To accompany stews, different farinaceous dishes are served in Hungary, often replacing potatoes and vegetables. These are always prepared at home, but if for some reason English housewives and cooks find it inconvenient to prepare the noodles, etc., they may be substituted by stewed rice, macaroni, and other products, available almost everywhere.

GALUSKA. I
(Small dumplings)

Cream 2 oz. lard (or butter), mix with 2 eggs, $\frac{1}{2}$ lb. flour, a pinch of salt and add—a little at a time—1 pint of milk. Beat the dough with a wooden spoon for about 10 minutes. By this time it will slip readily off the spoon. Prepare in a deep saucepan boiling salted water. Place the dough on a wet pastry-board, hold this close to the boiling water; with a small coffee-spoon, cut off small bits of the dough and drop them into the boiling water, dipping the spoon into the water frequently to prevent sticking. Boil these small pellets for 10 minutes, drain and hold them under running cold water. Drain again, and just before serving, toss them in $1\frac{1}{2}$ oz. melted butter. Sprinkle with salt and serve. This is a favourite garnish to accompany stews. It is also used to prepare many savoury puddings. (See under " Savoury Puddings.")

GALUSKA. II
(Small dumplings of puff-paste)

The same garnish as above, but prepared in a different way, and preferred by many people, who dislike a floury taste in garnish.
Prepare a chou-paste by melting in a saucepan 2 oz. lard, together with $\frac{1}{2}$ pint water; stir in—a little at a time—$\frac{1}{2}$ lb. flour. When it is smooth and readily slips off the spoon, take off the fire and let it get cold; blend carefully with 2 whipped eggs. Cook in exactly the same way as described above, but they will need a little less boiling in the salted water than " Galuska," prepared by the above method.

TARHONYA
(*Egg-barley*)

This tiny pearl-like pastry is sold in many stores abroad, but most Hungarian housewives prepare it at home. Tarhonya is probably one of the dried foods which the nomad Magyar tribes used to prepare in order to carry with them on their long rides, and their descendants still dry paste in the sun, bacon and meat in the chimney. Agricultural labourers and shepherds on the Puszta even in these days carry with them such dried food so that they can prepare a meal quickly over a bonfire. Below is given the method of preparing the pastry, and then the method to prepare the garnish.

Pastry. Mix thoroughly ½ lb. flour, 1 egg and just enough cold water to prepare a very stiff, hard pastry; spread out and let it dry thoroughly, then rub it through a coarse grater, to form small barley-shaped pearls. Spread these on baking sheets and dry either in the sun (as it is done in Hungary) or in an almost cool oven. Fill it into a linen bag and keep until required.

Garnish. Fry in 2 oz. melted lard or butter ½ lb. of " tarhonya," until a golden yellow colour is obtained, then sprinkle with ½ teaspoonful paprika and add enough stock (or water) to just cover; stew the egg-barley until tender, which takes 30 to 40 minutes, according to the size of the tarhonya pearls; by this time all the liquid should have disappeared. Season with salt and stir in 1½ oz. melted butter, shaking the pan to prevent burning. The tarhonya should be of a dark brown colour by the time it is ready. Suitable to accompany every Hungarian stew.

ZSEMLYE GOMBÓC
(*Savoury dumplings*)

Cut 2 large rolls, or 6 slices white bread into small dice. Dry them for a few minutes under grill or in oven, then fry lightly together with 1 teaspoonful chopped shallots in lard or dripping, adding a small quantity of chopped parsley. Squash with spoon and add 2 whole eggs, a few spoonfuls milk and enough flour to make a firm dough. Season with salt, form into dumplings (about 2½ in. in diameter), cook in salted, boiling water, drain and serve to accompany stews or cabbage-dishes.

SAVOURIES

Savouries, as they are known in England, are not so general in Hungary. Their place is taken by savoury puddings or "tészta" (see under this heading). However, they are not unknown, and the most popular are "Kukorica" and "Liptói"; these two are known far beyond the boundaries of Hungary.

KUKORICA
(*Sweet corn*)

Take as many sweet corn-cobs as required. Select those with white, tender corns, having a bluish-white colour. Remove leaves and hair, plunge them into deep, boiling salted water and cook for 15 to 20 minutes, according to age and size of the cobs. Lift them out, drain and arrange on folded napkin. At the table, each person should sprinkle the selected cob with salt, spread a little butter over it, take each end between the index and thumb, and eat it—turning it round and round. The season for young and tender corn-cobs in Hungary is July and August. Sweet corn is sold in recent years almost everywhere, both fresh and tinned.

LIPTÓI
(*Savoury cheese*)

Liptói is a cream cheese prepared of goats' milk; Liptói is sold in Hungary packed in small bladders and owes its name to the county of " Liptó " (now Czechoslovakia); this cheese has a peculiar acid flavour and is always served as " Körözött Liptói," or garnished cheese.

Take ½ lb. of good, sour cream cheese (curd), cream it with ½ lb. butter, season with ½ teaspoonful paprika, ½ teaspoonful chopped caraway seed, ½ teaspoonful mustard powder, a few chopped capers, ½ teaspoonful chopped chive or spring onion. Mix in a little ale or beer. When all is well blended and the mixture has a reddish-pink colour, pile high on a dish, garnish with radishes and serve with thin slices of brown bread. The German name of this cheese, " Liptauer," is often used in shops and restaurants both in Hungary and abroad, and it is sold under this name in England.

SAVOURY PUDDINGS

"TESZTA" or sweets play an important part in the Hungarian menu, and as explained at the beginning of this book, tészta does not necessarily mean pastry or pudding flavoured with sugar, but is very often a savoury dish. It is with the latter that this chapter is concerned. The following recipes are for dishes which may be used after the meat course, instead of the usual sweets, or as entrée dishes for a longer menu.

ANGYAL BÖGYÖLÖ
(Angels' food)

Prepare the pastry as described for " Káposztás Metélt " (Cabbage noodles) and cut it into 1-in. thick strips; if more convenient, use macaroni—if possible the flat variety. Boil the noodles in lightly salted water, drain and mix with 2 oz. melted butter, pile high on a warm dish and sprinkle with 4 oz. fine breadcrumbs, previously browned in about 2 oz. butter or lard.

This is a peasant dish and a great favourite in cottage kitchens.

GOMBÁS PALACSINTA
(Mushroom pancakes)

Prepare a batter by beating with a fork 3 eggs, 1 pint milk and a pinch of salt; add ½ lb. flour and fry in the usual way 12 large, very thin, pancakes. Spread on each pancake a layer of stewed mushrooms, roll in tightly (like a Swiss roll), sprinkle top with salt and melted butter, place under the grill for a minute, just before serving. For the stewed mushrooms, clean and slice 1 lb. mushrooms, fry lightly in butter together with 1 teaspoonful chopped shallots, add a little thick cream; season with salt and paprika. Keep warm until wanted.

KÁPOSZTÁS METÉLT
(Noodles with cabbage)

Prepare a very firm, dry pastry by mixing 10 oz. sieved flour, 2 eggs, a pinch of salt and enough water to moisten the mixture. Knead the pastry until quite firm, divide into 3 or 4 balls and leave it in cold place for a few hours to dry. Then roll out rather thinly, cut it into $\frac{1}{2}$-in. broad strips and then again crosswise, to obtain small, square, flat pieces of pastry; throw into boiling, salted water, cook for 10 minutes, drain and hold them under the cold-water tap to prevent sticking. Meanwhile 1 small, shredded cabbage should be fried in 3 oz. lard, together with 1 oz. chopped onion and a pinch of salt and paprika. Add a little water and stew until tender. Mix cabbage and noodles thoroughly, serve very hot. Season with freshly ground pepper.

SONKÁS GALUSKA
(Pellets with ham)

Prepare as in Tojásos Galuska (Pellets with eggs) but instead of eggs, use 6 or 7 oz. chopped ham.

SONKÁS METÉLT
(Noodles with ham)

Prepare the noodles in exactly the same way as described in recipe for " Káposztás Metélt " ; after draining the noodles, place into a saucepan together with 2 oz. melted butter and $\frac{1}{2}$ lb. cooked, chopped ham. Mix thoroughly over gentle heat, shaking the pan to prevent burning. As soon as the noodles are sufficiently warm, serve, piled on a dish.

SONKÁS PALACSINTA
(Pancakes with ham)

Bake 12 thin pancakes, as described in " Gombás Palacsinta " ; keep them hot, spread on them finely chopped, cooked ham, roll and place under grill for a minute. For 12 pancakes, about $\frac{1}{2}$ lb. cooked chopped ham.

TOJÁSOS GALUSKA
(Pellets with eggs)

Prepare the small dumplings, as described in the recipes for " Galuska " in Chapter " Garnish " ; either of the two recipes may be used. Drain the Galuska, hold under cold-water tap for a minute, drain again. Melt in a stewpan 2 oz. butter, mix in the Galuska and add a mixture of 3 well-beaten eggs and 1 spoonful thick cream, shaking the pan. As soon as the eggs are set and well mixed with the pellets, season with salt and serve, piled high on a warm dish.

TÚRÓS CSUSZA
(*Noodles with cheese*)

Prepare and cook the same quantity and shape of noodles as described in recipe for " Káposztás Metélt." Mix with 3 oz. melted lard, 10 oz. sour cream cheese, 1 gill sour cream and 3 oz. fat, uncured bacon, previously chopped and fried golden brown. Serve very hot.

SAVOURY ROLLS
(RÉTESEK)

GOMBÁS RÉTES
(*Mushroom roll*)

PREPARE the pastry, as described in recipe for "Almás rétes" (see SWEETS). For the filling stew 4 oz. mushrooms, with a little chopped onion and parsley, mix it into a creamy Béchamel and cook slowly until it is rather thick ; take off the fire and stir in 3 egg-yolks and the stiffly whisked whites of 3 eggs. Spread this mixture on the thin "rétes" pastry, roll very loosely, place on greased baking sheet, brush with melted butter and bake in moderate oven golden brown. To be served warm, cut slantwise into slices, either as an entrée dish or savoury.

KÁPOSZTÁS RÉTES
(*Cabbage roll*)

Same method as "Mushroom roll," but for filling use 1 small cabbage, shredded and fried in about 3 oz. lard, seasoned with salt, pepper and a pinch of paprika.

SAJTOS RÉTES
(*Cheese roll*)

Same method as above, but instead of the mushrooms, grated cheese—according to taste—is stirred into the Béchamel.

SONKÁS RÉTES
(*Ham roll*)

Same method as Mushroom roll, but use very finely minced ham.

SWEETS

IN this chapter are given recipes for the best known and most popular sweet " Tészta," many of which will sound quaint to those unacquainted with Hungarian cookery, but all of which deserve trying.

ALMÁS RÉTES
(*Apple roll*)

" Rétes " is a flaky pastry, extremely thin, and its preparation requires at least four hands ; it is considered the queen of " tésztas " and to be an expert in this art is the ambition of every Hungarian cook.

Pile $\frac{1}{2}$ lb. of the finest Hungarian flour (containing 13 per cent. albumen and 65 per cent. starch) on a wooden board, make a deepening in the middle. Mix in a bowl a few spoonfuls of lukewarm water with a pinch of salt, 1 small egg, 1 oz. of butter and add this mixture—little by little—to the flour, pouring it into the deepening and working the pastry first with a spoon, then with the hands. Knead rapidly and thoroughly until a smooth and pliable dough is obtained ; place in a slightly heated bowl, cover with serviette and let it stand at least ½ hour. Place a large table in the middle of the kitchen, cover with clean cloth, sprinkle the cloth with flour, place the pastry on top and roll out with a specially long and narrow rolling-pin as thin as possible ; brush the pastry thinly with melted lard or butter and now two or three persons should pull the pastry in all directions, until transparent, taking great care to avoid cracks and holes. Cut away the thick edges, brush again with melted butter, sprinkle with breadcrumbs (previously fried in butter), thin slices of peeled and cored apples (about 2 lbs.), 3 oz. sugar and 2 oz. sultanas. Roll by lifting the tablecloth gently, place on greased baking tin, brush top with melted butter, and bake in warm oven until brown. Sprinkle with castor sugar before serving and cut slantwise into 3-in. thick slices. The pastry should be as thin and crisp as a wafer.

ALMÁS PITÉ
(*Apple tart*)

Work into a smooth pastry 12 oz. flour, 8 oz. butter, 3 oz. sugar, 1 gill cream, a little lemon juice, 1 spoonful brandy and a pinch of salt (if salted butter is used, the salt must be eliminated). Divide the pastry into two equal parts, roll out both the size and shape of your baking tin, line the latter with pastry and bake it lightly. Meanwhile peel and core 2 lbs. cider apples, cut into very thin slices, mix with 2 oz. chopped nuts, 1 oz. sultanas, a little brandy and season with cinnamon and sugar to taste. Spread this mixture on baked pastry, cover with other half of pastry, brush top with egg and bake in moderate oven until golden brown. Cut into wedge, or square, pieces.

ALMÁS RIZS
(*Rice pudding with apples*)

Boil in 2 pints milk 7 oz. rice ; let it get cold. Meanwhile cream 4 oz. butter, 2½ oz. castor sugar, add the grated rind of ½ lemon, 4 egg-yolks and the cold rice ; lastly fold in the beaten whites of 4 eggs. Turn ⅓ of this mixture into a buttered, fireproof mould, place on it a layer of 1 lb. peeled, cored, thinly sliced apples, sprinkle liberally with sugar, turn in the rest of the rice mixture, sprinkle top with sugar and melted butter and bake in oven for about 20 minutes. Serve in same dish.

Many other fruits may be used instead of apples, such as halved apricots, peaches, stoned cherries, etc. The pudding may be steamed, instead of baked, in which case the mixture is filled into a pudding mould, closed carefully and steamed for 45 to 50 minutes. Turn out and serve with suitable fruit sauce.

CSERESZNYÉS RÉTES
(Cherry roll)

Prepare rétes as described in "Almás rétes" recipe ; instead of apples, use 3 lbs. stoned cherries.

CSÖRÖGE
(Fancy Doughnuts)

Dissolve a teaspoonful yeast in a little lukewarm milk, work into 1 pint of fine flour, 2 oz. sugar and 1 oz. butter. If sweet butter is used, a little salt must be added. Add 3 egg yolks and beat with spoon until a smooth dough is obtained; let it rise in warm place for at least 1 hour. With a wheeled cutter cut the pastry into square pieces, about 3 in. in diameter, and cut into the middle two incisions, which must not reach the edges. Twist into fancy shapes and drop them into boiling lard. When golden brown lift them out, drain and sprinkle with castor sugar, flavoured with vanilla. Serve hot, accompanied by fruit sauce or jam.

FAHÉJAS BURGONYAFÁNK
(Potato doughnuts)

Bake some large, white and floury potatoes in their jackets, peel and press through sieve. For 2 oz. potatoes, take 4 oz. butter, 1 oz. yeast (dissolved in milk), 1 oz. sugar, 2 oz. flour, 4 egg yolks and a pinch of salt. Work into a smooth dough, beat with wooden spoon until light and let it rise in a warm place for 1 hour. Roll out about ½ in.

thick, cut into rounds about 2½ in. in diameter, let them rise again, then drop the rounds into deep, boiling lard, drain and serve sprinkled with cinnamon and castor sugar.

DIÓS METÉLT
(Noodles with nuts)

Prepare pastry as described in "Káposztás metélt." After draining the noodles, shake them with 2 oz. melted butter, mix with 6-8 oz. grated nuts and sprinkle with castor sugar.

FORGÁCSFÁNK
(Fancy doughnuts)

Similar to "Csöröge," but the doughnuts are cut into pieces 2 inches broad and 3½ inches long, making two or three incisions in the middle, length-wise, without reaching the edges. Fry and serve like "Csöröge."

GESZTENYE FELFUJT
(Chestnut pudding)

Roast or grill 1½ lbs. chestnuts, then peel and press through wire sieve. Place into a saucepan the peeled and mashed chestnuts, together with 2 gills milk, 6 oz. sugar, 3 to 4 oz. grated nuts and cook slowly for ¼ hour, then cool and add 2 oz. butter, 5 egg-yolks and lastly the stiffly whisked whites of 5 eggs. Turn into greased and dusted pudding mould, close and steam for 45 minutes. Turn out and serve with whipped cream.

GESZTENYE CSEMEGE
(Chestnut trifle)

Roast, peel and mash 1½ lbs. chestnuts, sweeten to taste and flavour with brandy or vanilla. Place into suitable bowl layerwise with red-currant jam and grated chocolate, decorate top with whipped cream, into which a little jam is mixed to make it pink. Serve ice-cold.

61

GESZTENYE KRÉM
(*Chestnut trifle*)

Roast and peel 1½ lbs. chestnuts, but do not mash. Place the peeled chestnuts into a bowl, together with coarsely chopped candied fruit (about ½ lb.) and 1 oz. Malaga raisins. Cover with 1 pint good egg custard and decorate top with whipped cream.

GESZTENYE PÜRÉE
(*Chestnut cream*)

Boil for 10 minutes 1½ lb. chestnuts, then remove outer and inner peel, place into saucepan, covered with milk; boil gently until quite soft, then press through wire sieve. Boil quickly 2 gills water and the same quantity of sugar until syrupy, but not brown, mix quickly with the mashed chestnuts and flavour with vanilla. Cool and then mix with 2 gills whipped cream. Pile high on a suitable plate and decorate with whipped cream. Serve ice-cold.

KOSSUTH TÉSZTA
(*Yeast cakes with jam*)

Kossuth, the leader of the Revolution of 1848, and a national hero, has given his name to many Hungarian dishes.
Rub 1 lb. fine flour with ½ lb. butter; add 6 egg-yolks, ½ oz. dissolved yeast, 1½ oz. castor sugar and a pinch of salt. Work into a smooth dough, let it rise in warm place, then roll out ¼ in. thick, place on greased tin, cover with ½ in. layer of red currant or other jam and bake. Cut into large, square pieces and serve warm or cold.

LOBOGÓ
(*Flaming soufflé*)

Beat until stiff the white of 5 eggs, then fold in carefully 2 oz. grated chocolate, 3 oz. castor sugar. Meanwhile cook 3 oz. Malaga raisins in a few spoonfuls brandy or rum, then place them in shallow, fireproof dish, cover with the above mixture and bake in hot oven for a few minutes. Pour sugared brandy or rum over the soufflé, light and take quickly to serve. It may be lighted in the dining-room.

MÁKOS CSUSZA
(*Noodles with poppy seeds*)

Poppy seeds are very popular in Hungary to use as filling or sprinkling " tészta." Make a noodle pastry, as described in " Káposztás Metélt," cut into flat strips about ½ in. broad and 3 in. long, boil, drain and mix with 2 oz. melted butter, 3 oz. pounded poppy seeds (the dark variety), and sprinkle with 2 oz. sugar. In many Hungarian families honey is used instead of sugar; in the latter case, less butter is sufficient.

MEGGYES LEPÉNY
(*Cherry tart*)

Prepare a similar pastry as described for " Kossuth tészta," roll out and cover with sour cherry (morella) jam; place a pastry-trellis over it, brush with egg, sprinkle with coarse sugar and chopped almonds and bake.

PALACSINTA
(*Pancakes*)

Pancakes form the basis of many sweets; the quantity given in this recipe for the batter is enough for 12 thin pancakes, about 10 in. in diameter.

Make a smooth, rather thin batter of 6 oz. flour, 2 eggs, salt, 1 pint milk, 1½ oz. castor sugar; 1 teaspoonful of beer, wine or brandy is optional, but helps to make the pancakes crisp. Heat up thoroughly a thick iron or copper pan, melt a little lard and butter in it and pour 1 large spoonful of the batter in the middle of the pan, shaking it so that the batter should thinly cover the whole surface. Fry, loosening the edges with an omelette knife, toss on other side and fry. Keep the pancakes warm until wanted. It is always best to prepare them as late as possible.

PALACSINTA FELFUJT
(*Pancake soufflé*)

Prepare the pancakes as described above, cut them into ½ in. thick strips, mix with 2 oz. grated almonds or nuts, 2 oz. raisins and 1 oz. coarse sugar; place the mixture into a buttered fireproof dish. Whisk the whites of 3 eggs until stiff, fold in 2 spoonfuls castor sugar, 3 spoonfuls apricot or other jam, turn on top of the pancakes and bake in oven until the froth has become firm, which takes about 10 minutes in moderate oven.

RAKOTT PALACSINTA
(Baked pancakes)

Prepare the pancakes, cut them into ½ in. thick strips, mix with 2 spoonfuls jam, 2 oz. sultanas, 3 oz. grated nuts, place into buttered fireproof dish and bake in oven for a few minutes.

TEJFELES PALACSINTA
(Pancakes with cream)

Prepare 12 thin pancakes, as described, brush each with thick sweet cream, sprinkle with grated almonds, chopped sultanas and currants, roll them tightly, place on buttered baking tin, brush top with cream and bake for a few minutes in moderate oven.

TÚRÓS PALACSINTA
(Pancakes with cream cheese)

Prepare 12 pancakes, spread on them the following cream, roll tightly, brush with butter, sprinkle with castor sugar, and grill them for a minute before serving. Cream: Mix 2 oz. butter, 1½ oz. sugar, ½ gill thick, sweet cream, ½ lb. sweet cream cheese (curd), 2 oz. sultanas, 2 eggs.

TÚRÓS GOMBÓC
(Curd dumplings)

" Túró " is the Hungarian name for sweet cream cheese, a soft curd, used in many dishes. If not available in shops, it may be prepared at home with the help of junket tablets. To each quart of fresh milk add 1 junket tablet, leave the milk in warm place for ½ hour, then place in cheese cloth, hang up over sink to drain for a night. Press 1 lb. of curd through wire sieve, mix with 3 egg yolks, 1 oz. butter, 2 oz. flour, the stiffly beaten whites of 3 eggs and 1½ oz. sugar. Form into dumplings, throw them into boiling, lightly salted water, cook for 6 to 8 minutes, drain and roll them in a mixture of cinnamon and castor sugar. Instead of the latter, they may be rolled in breadcrumbs, previously fried in butter.

TÚRÓS PÁSTÉTOM
(*Curd pudding*)

Press through wire sieve 1 lb. sweet cream cheese, mix with 3 oz. semolina, 3 oz. sultanas, a little grated lemon-peel, 6 oz. sugar, 5 egg-yolks and fold in carefully the stiffly whisked whites of the 5 eggs. Turn the mixture into greased pudding mould and steam for 1½ hours. Serve with egg custard.

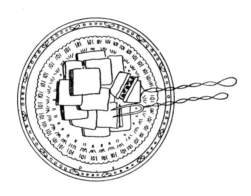

CAKES

THE number of recipes for delicious Hungarian cakes is legion, and a complete collection of them would fill a book. Every family has a number of closely guarded, inherited recipes; those given below are for the most popular and well-known cakes. Hungarian cooks, as already mentioned, are dexterous pastry-makers, but the work is made comparatively easy by the wonderful, light, dry Hungarian flour, known far beyond the boundaries of the country. Mrs. Beeton's famous cookery book recommends its use for pastry-making, and it is used by professional bakers all over Europe.

Similarly to " tészta," Hungarian cakes are often savoury cakes; for example, the cakes and biscuits served with wine are almost always flavoured with salt and not with sugar.

It will be observed that most cakes are called " torta " which means layer-cake, usually iced, but " torta " may also mean a large tart.

The preparation of some of the cakes involves considerable work and takes time; for this reason, in the recipes for such cakes, the quantity given will be enough for ten to twelve persons, as it is considered a waste of time and material to prepare such cakes in small quantity.

The following recipes, tested by generations of housewives, are urgently recommended and well worth the trouble of trying, as nothing brings more satisfaction to hostesses, housewives and cooks, than successful cakes.

ALMA TORTA
(*Apple tart*)

Rub 7 oz. butter into ½ lb. sifted, fine flour, then work in 1 egg, 2 oz. sugar and the grated rind of ½ lemon; let the pastry rest for 1 hour. After this time, roll out the pastry on a floured board, cut into 3 equal size rounds, prick them with a fork and bake for 10 minutes in moderate oven. Meanwhile cook 3 lbs. cider apples to pulp, press through sieve, cook again for a few minutes with 2 or 3 oz. sugar, mix with 1 oz. raisins, 2 oz. apricot jam and a little grated lemon-peel. Spread this apple cream on two rounds of the pastry, covering each other; cover with third. Brush top with milk, sprinkle with sugar and bake in oven for ½ hour. Serve lukewarm, cut into wedge-shaped pieces. It may be also served cold.

BURGONYA TORTA
(*Potato cake*)

Grate finely 7 oz. cooked, floury potatoes, then mix with 2 oz. sweet, and a few bitter, grated almonds, 2 oz. sugar, a little grated lemon peel, 2 whole eggs, 4 egg-yolks, and cream this mixture for at least 20 minutes;

then add carefully the stiffly whisked whites of the 4 eggs, put the mixture into a buttered cake mould and bake in very moderate oven. When cold, cut across into 3 rounds, fill the spaces between the layers with jam and ice with almond icing.

CSOKOLÁDÉ KENYÉR
(*Chocolate bread*)

Whip 4 eggs, mix with 5 oz. castor sugar, 5 oz. grated chocolate, 1½ oz. grated nuts, 2½ oz. flour, turn the mixture into a buttered, loaf-shaped mould and bake in moderate oven. When cold, cover with chocolate icing and serve cut into slices.

CSOKOLÁDÉ SZELET
(*Chocolate cakes*)

Cream ½ lb. each of butter, sugar, melted chocolate and flour, add 6 egg-yolks and lastly 6 whipped egg-whites, spread ½ in. thick on a buttered flat baking tin and bake in warm oven. When cold, cut into squares or rounds, set two and two together with jam between and cover with chocolate icing.

CSOKOLÁDÉ TORTA
(*Chocolate layercake*)

Cream 3 oz. butter with 5 oz. sugar, 6 egg-yolks, 3 oz. unpeeled, grated almonds, 5 oz. grated chocolate, 2 oz. very fine, sifted dry breadcrumbs ; when everything is thoroughly mixed, which should take at least 20 minutes, fold in the stiffly whisked whites of the 6 eggs. Bake in two large, round cake-tins, carefully brushed with melted butter. When cold, cut across each round, to make four uniform layers, fill with chocolate cream and cover with chocolate icing. Cream: 6 oz. unsalted butter creamed with 2 egg-yolks, 4 oz. melted chocolate and 2 oz. sugar. Icing: boil until thick 3½ oz. lump sugar with 2 spoonfuls water, then add 3 oz. melted chocolate and a little piece of sweet butter; when it covers a silver spoon, pour over the filled cake, without touching it with knife or spoon. It will spread evenly, if the icing is hot. Touching it spoils the shiny appearance of the icing and gives it a dull, amateurish look.

DIÓS TORTA
(*Nut layercake*)

Beat with fork 7 egg-yolks, then add 5 oz. castor sugar, 3 oz. each of walnuts and almonds (both grated with the brown skin); cream the mixture for 15 to 20 minutes, then fold in the stiffly whisked whites of the 7 eggs. Bake in two round buttered cake-tins and, when cold, cut each across, to form four layers. Place the rounds on top of each other, filled with the following cream : Cream 6 oz. sweet butter with 6 oz. sugar, 1 egg-yolk and ½ gill very strong mocca coffee (made with 1 oz. mocca and very little boiling water). Cover the filled cake with coffee icing, made by boiling until thick 7 oz. lump sugar with 1 gill water, then adding 7 oz. icing sugar and 2-3 spoonfuls very strong mocca coffee. Decorate the cake with halved, iced walnuts.

DOBOS TORTA
(*Drum cake*)

This is a very famous cake and requires great care in making.

Beat with fork 6 egg yolks, then add 6 oz. castor sugar, 4 oz. flour and fold in carefully the beaten whites of the 6 eggs. Brush with melted butter 6 uniform round cake tins, dust with flour and spread the batter rather thinly on these cake tins. Bake in moderate oven until biscuit-coloured and take them off carefully, whilst warm. When they are cold, spread on 5 layers the following cream:—Add 4 oz. melted choco-late to 8 oz. creamed, sweet butter, 8 oz. sugar and 1 egg-yolk. Place the layers on top of each other, with layers of the cream between, trim the edge of the cake, cover with the last cake layer and with caramel icing, prepared by boiling 3 oz. icing sugar, stirring until a deep brown colour is obtained; pour it quickly over the surface of the cake, without smoothing it with knife or spoon; it will stiffen straight-away. Cut into very thin slices 1 oz. almonds, grill them slightly and cover the sides of the cake with these slices, overlapping each other.

This cake takes a lot of trouble, but will be found worth while; the waferlike layers of pastry alternating with the cream, the bitter-sweet taste of the icing make it one of the most delicious of cakes.

ERZSÉBET TORTA
(*Elisabeth cake*)

Named after Queen Elisabeth of Hungary, this was her favourite cake. Beat 2 whole eggs, 4 egg-yolks, 5 oz. sugar, add 5 oz. grated and 1 oz. shredded almonds, 1 oz. cake- or fine breadcrumbs and 4 whipped egg-whites. Bake in 2 buttered round cake moulds; when cold, cut across and fill with egg custard (4 yolks, 3 spoonfuls ground rice, ½ pint cream, sugar, vanilla or almond to flavour). Cover the cake with white sugar icing.

FORGÁCS TEKERCS
(*Stuffed rolls*)

Whip 3 eggs with a fork, add 5 oz. castor sugar, a little vanilla and lastly fold in 3 oz. flour. Spread on buttered and floured cake tin rather thinly, bake until set, cut into 1-in. broad and 10-in. long strips, fold them quickly round the handle of a wooden spoon to form hollow tubes. Slip off as soon as stiff. Continue until all the pastry is used; it must be done quickly, best by several persons. Just before serving, fill them with whipped cream, into which a little Kirsch or other liqueur is mixed. They may also be filled with egg custard.

GESZTENYE TORTA
(*Chestnut cake*)

Take 1 lb. cooked and peeled chestnuts, mash and press through sieve; mix now with 10 oz. castor sugar, 6 yolks and 6 whipped egg-whites; lastly add 3 oz. grated almonds. Brush a round cake mould with butter, dust with flour, pour in the mixture and bake in moderate oven. Try with pin, if ready. When cold, cut across to make two or three layers, fill with sweetened whipped cream and decorate top also with whipped cream.

HUNYADI TORTA
(*Cake named after the national hero Hunyadi János, 1387-1456*)

One whole egg, 6 yolks are well beaten and then mixed with 5 oz. each of sugar and grated nuts, 1 oz. grated chocolate, 1½ oz. cake-crumbs or fine breadcrumbs; fold in carefully the stiffly whipped whites of 6 eggs. Turn the mixture into 2 large buttered and dusted cake tins, bake in moderate oven. When cold, cut across to make four layers, fill with red-currant jelly, ice with chocolate icing and decorate with ½ pint sweetened whipped cream.

HUSZÁR FÁNK
(Hussar cakes)

Rub 4 oz. butter with 5 oz. flour, add 2 oz. sugar and 2 yolks. Work into smooth pastry, form into small balls, place them on buttered baking sheet; with the handle of a wooden spoon, press small deepenings into the middle of each ball, brush them with egg-white, sprinkle with chopped almonds and coarse sugar and bake in moderate oven light brown. Before serving, fill the cavity in each cake with red currant jam.

KOSSUTH KARIKÁK
(Kossuth ringlets)

These cakes are named after Kossuth, a famous Hungarian statesman and political leader of the Revolution of 1848.
Rub ½ lb. butter into ½ lb. flour, work with 3 yolks and 3 oz. sugar into smooth pastry, if necessary add a few spoonfuls milk. Divide the pastry into 2 equal parts; mix into one part of the pastry 1 oz. grated chocolate. Form of both the white and dark pastry strips about ½ in. broad and 7 in. long, twist one brown and one white together, form into ringlets, place them on greased baking sheets, brush with egg-white and bake in moderate oven.

MÁKOS PATKÓ
(Poppy seed horseshoe)

" Poppy seed horseshoe " is a literary translation of this cake; it is the traditional Hungarian Christmas cake and is actually shaped as a large horseshoe to bring luck. Usually a large quantity is made, to last until New Year, and is offered with wine, tea or coffee to visitors, cut into 1-in. slanting slices.

Dissolve 1 oz. yeast in a few spoonfuls fresh cream and work into 10 oz. flour, 6 oz. butter, 1 egg and 3 yolks, 2 oz. sugar and a little cream. Beat with wooden spoon until light and flexible; let it rise for a few hours in a not too warm place. Then place the pastry on a floured board, divide into 6 pieces and roll each piece out to an oblong, about 8 in. wide and 15 to 16 in. long. Spread on them the poppy seed mixture, roll in rather tightly, form into horseshoe, let it rise again, brush with egg and bake. Filling: 1 pint poppy seed boiled in ½ pint milk, together with chopped lemon peel, 1 oz. raisins, 3 oz. sugar, 2 oz. butter. Cool, and keep until wanted.

MÁKOS RÉTES
(*Poppy seed roll*)

Dissolve ½ oz. yeast in ½ gill milk, work into a dough made of 4 oz. butter, ½ lb. flour, 1 oz. sugar and a pinch of salt. Beat with spoon, then cover and let it rise, which will take at least 1 hour. Meanwhile boil 1 pint dark poppy seeds in ½ pint milk, with 1 oz. currants, a teaspoonful cinnamon and 2½ to 3 oz. sugar, take off the fire and add 2 oz. butter. Let it get cold. Roll out the pastry rather thinly, spread on it the poppy-seed mixture, roll in, place on baking sheet and let it rise again for ½ hour. Brush with milk, sprinkle with sugar and bake golden brown. Serve warm or cold, cut into slanting, 1-in. thick slices. This cake will not keep so long as the " Patkó."

MAGYAR TORTA
(*Hungarian layercake*)

Rub 10 oz. flour with 4 oz. butter, add 3 oz. sugar, 5 oz. unpeeled, grated nuts or almonds, 2 eggs and some grated lemon peel. Brush with butter a large, round cake mould (the sides should be at least 4 in. high), dust with flour and line bottom and sides of the mould with the rolled out pastry. Prick with fork and bake for a few minutes to make firm. The cake is filled first with apple filling, then with poppy seed filling, lastly with nut filling. Decorate top with strips of the pastry (trimmings) to resemble sunrays, brush with egg, sprinkle with chopped almonds and bake for 1½ hours.

Apple filling : Stew 6 large peeled and cored apples with sugar, sultanas and a little brandy. It should be a rather firm mash.

Poppy seed filling : (same as described in recipe for "Mákos rétes.").

Nut filling: Boil, until thick, 5 oz. sugar with 1 gill water, then add 10 oz. grated walnuts. Take off the fire and mix with 1 oz. sweet butter.

MOGYORÓ TORTA
(Hazelnut cake)

Beat 6 yolks and add to them 6 tablespoonfuls sugar, the juice of $\frac{1}{2}$ lemon, $3\frac{1}{2}$ oz. grated hazelnuts and 2 tablespoonfuls fine dried crumbs (of cake or white bread). Fold in the stiffly whisked whites of 6 eggs. Brush with butter and dust with flour a round cake-mould, turn the mixture in and bake in moderate oven. When cold, cut across into 3 layers. Meanwhile cook in $\frac{1}{2}$ pint milk 8 tablespoonfuls grated hazelnuts with 5 tablespoonfuls sugar ; when thick, take off the fire and let it get cold. Add now to this mixture 3 oz. sweet, creamed butter, 2 spoonfuls very strong mocca coffee and a little brandy. Spread the cream between the layers and with rest decorate top. Sprinkle top with grilled, chopped nuts. Serve cold.

MORZSA TORTA
(Crumb cake)

There are from time to time in every household dry pieces of plain cakes, such as sponge, etc., left over. These should be kept in closed tin, and crushed when wanted. To 4 oz. cake crumbs, add 6 yolks, $\frac{1}{2}$ lb. flour, a little cinnamon or vanilla to flavour and 2 oz. creamed butter. When all is very well mixed, fold in the stiffly whisked egg-whites of the 6 eggs. Turn into greased cake mould, cut across when baked and cold, fill with jam and decorate with whipped cream and chopped almonds.

POZSONYI KIFLI
(Pressbourg cakes)

Pozsony, Hungary's old coronation town, now belonging to Czecho-slovakia, is famous for its pastrycooks.

Prepare smooth pastry by mixing 4 oz. butter, 8 oz. flour, 1 oz. sugar,

$\frac{1}{2}$ oz. dissolved yeast and 1 yolk ; let it rise for 1 hour, then roll out and cut into 3-in. wide and 4$\frac{1}{2}$-in. long pieces. Spread on each nut-cream (described in " Magyar torta "), roll them tightly and bend into horseshoe shapes ; let them rise, brush with egg and stretch them a little. Bake. (The stretching causes them to have a marble-like pattern, when baked.)

POGÁCSA
(Round cakes)

" Pogácsa " is the name for several small cakes, salted and sweet, served with wine or tea. Hungarian hostesses serve wine to morning callers; wine is also served instead of cocktails and it is on such occasions that pogácsa accompany the drink.

Burgonyás pogácsa (potato cakes). 5 oz. cooked, floury potatoes, 5 oz. flour, 4 oz. butter, 1 yolk and a little baking powder, worked into smooth pastry, rolled out about 1$\frac{1}{2}$ in. thick, cut into small, round cakes, 2 in. in diameter, brushed with egg, sprinkled with sugar and baked.

Töpörtyüs pogácsa (savoury cakes with bacon cracklings). Take 1 lb. unsalted, uncured (fresh) bacon, cut it into small dice, wash well, place them in an iron pan and fry on brisk fire, adding a few spoonsful milk, to prevent burning. Take care to stir the whole time ; when the dice are a golden colour, take off the fire, drain, but do not press them (the lard may be used separately). These fried bacon dice or cracklings are called " töpörtyü " in Hungarian. Chop finely $\frac{1}{2}$ lb. cold " töpörtyü," rub into 10 oz. flour, add $\frac{1}{2}$ gill each of cream and white wine, 2 yolks, a pinch of salt, 1 oz. dissolved yeast. Roll out and fold several times, just as flaky pastry, resting the pastry in cold place between the folding process. When this is done 3 to 4 times, roll out 1 in. thick, cut into round pieces, about 2$\frac{1}{2}$ in. in diameter, place them on greased baking sheet, brush top with egg, sprinkle with coarse salt and chopped caraway seed and bake in warm oven golden brown. As they should rise in the oven take care when brushing that the egg should not run down the sides. These cakes are considered the best to accompany wine.

Vajas pogácsa (butter cakes). Rub 5 oz. butter into 6 oz. flour, mix with 4 oz. sugar, a little vanilla, 1 egg-yolk ; roll out 1 in. thick, cut into small rounds, brush with egg, sprinkle with chopped almonds and bake. All cakes called " pogácsa " resemble somewhat " scones."

74

PÜSPÖKKENYÉR
(*Bishop's bread*)

Cream 5 oz. butter with 5 oz. sugar, add 5 yolks, 2 spoonfuls brandy, 1 oz. each of candied orange and lemon peel, 3 oz. peeled, shredded almonds, 1 oz. each of sultanas and currants ; lastly fold in 5 oz. flour and the stiffly beaten whites of 5 eggs. Brush with butter and dust with flour a long, loaf-shaped mould, turn into this the mixture and bake in moderate oven. If the flour is not self-raising, add a little baking powder. When cold, cut the cake into slices.

TÚRÓSBÉLES
(*Curd cakes*)

Prepare a flaky pastry of ½ lb. flour, 1 egg, 2 oz. sugar, ½ oz. yeast, a pinch of salt, roll out very thin. Work now 5 oz. butter with 2 oz. flour, cut into slices and work into rolled-out pastry. Roll out and fold together in the usual manner, resting the pastry in cool place between the folding process. Meanwhile cream 1 oz. butter with 2 oz. sugar, add 2 yolks, ½ lb. sweet cream cheese (curd), 3 spoonfuls thick cream, 1 oz. sultanas and either grated lemon peel or vanilla for flavouring. Roll out the pastry rather thin, cut into 4-in. squares with a heated knife, place a large spoonful of cream on each square, pinch the four corners together, place the cakes on greased sheet, brush with egg and bake.

TÚRÓS TORTA
(*Curd cake*)

Line a shallow, round tart mould with the following pastry : 3 oz. butter, 5 oz. flour, 2 oz. sugar, 2 yolks and a little grated lemon peel. Bake light brown, then fill with curd cream, prepared by mixing 2 oz. butter, 3 yolks, 2 oz. vanilla sugar, ½ lb. curd, 3 stiffly beaten egg-whites. Beat now 3 whole eggs, add 1 oz. melted, cold butter, 1 oz. sugar, 1 oz. flour. Spread this mixture on top of cake and bake in very moderate oven ½ hour.

N.B.—If the sweet cream cheese is not available, prepare as described in recipe for " Túrós Gombóc " (curd dumplings) on page 64.

VAJAS TORTA. I
(Butter cake)

Prepare double quantity of flaky pastry, as described in " Turósbéles," cut into 3 large rounds and bake. When cold, spread on each a thin layer of red currant jelly, a thick layer of good egg custard and decorate top with whipped cream.

VAJAS TORTA. II
(Butter cake)

Rub $\frac{1}{2}$ lb. butter into 1 lb. flour, add 5 yolks, 4 oz. sugar, a pinch of salt, a little brandy and enough cream to make a flexible, smooth pastry. Roll out $\frac{1}{4}$ in. thick, cut into 4 or 5 large, round pieces, bake them, and when cold, place on top of each other, filled between layers either with apple, nut or curd filling, described in other recipes.

VALÓDI TORDAI MÉZES
(Real Torda spice-cakes)

Boil 10 oz. honey, skim and cool, mix with 6 oz. rye flour and enough fine wheat flour to make a smooth pastry, which readily slips off the spoon. The flour should be previously sifted and mixed with a teaspoonful bicarbonate of soda and a small spoonful of allspice. Roll out the pastry rather thinly, place on a baking sheet, previously rubbed with beeswax and dusted with flour. Brush the pastry with a beaten egg, sprinkle with chopped almonds and bake in moderate oven. Cut, whilst still warm, into fancy shapes and keep in airtight biscuit-box until required. These cakes will keep a long time.

A FEW WORDS TO TRAVELLERS VISITING HUNGARY

A STEADILY increasing stream of English travellers visit Hungary each year, all of them anxious to see this beautiful country and to learn to know the strange but attractive ways of its people. The proverbial and truly oriental hospitality of the Hungarians makes this easy—everybody is anxious to show foreigners all the sights and proud to be of help.

To make a visit to Hungary a complete success and the unforgettable experience it ought to be, it is necessary to see as much as possible of the country, the peasants wearing picturesque costumes—different in

77

each village—try the many marvellous bathing establishments and thermal baths of Budapest and, last but not least, to sample the wonderful national cuisine, accompanied by Hungarian wines and fruit brandies.

As already mentioned, this book should serve English readers to enable them to prepare in their homes those Hungarian dishes for which the ingredients are easily available everywhere ; the cooking of such dishes will cause no difficulty even to inexperienced cooks. The wines mentioned in the Appendix are also available in England, both for home consumption and at certain restaurants ; this wine dictionary should help the readers to select suitable wines, either when ordering them in England, or when travelling on the Continent. There are many Hungarian restaurants outside Hungary.

First, I should like to advise the tourist when in Hungary to try to avoid the large and showy restaurants and grill-rooms. Such places are to be found everywhere, they are never very interesting. French food is better in France, the grill-rooms are better in England. Hungarian friends or the hotel porter will gladly supply the names and addresses of charming small or open-air restaurants, with real gipsy music and the best Hungarian cuisine—there are plenty to choose from, to suit the pocket of the rich, the well-to-do or of those whose means are more modest. They are all good—bad cooking is the great exception in Hungary and need not be feared, even in the most modest eating places, such as the simple riverside inns, frequented by all classes of people on Fridays for fish meals.

The next step should be to ask someone for the address of the nearest and best Transsylvanian restaurant, usually called " Erdélyi csárda " or " Erdélyi borozó " (Transsylvanian inn), and kept by emigrants—this lovely part of Hungary belonging now to Roumania. Transsylvania is as different from Hungary proper as Scotland is from England, and of all the regional cookeries its cuisine is one of the best and most original. Some of these specialities are very famous, but most of them were unknown, even in Hungary, before the emigrants started to popularise them in their charming little restaurants, where there usually is a very good menu, consisting of specialities. Even the most critical gourmet may safely order such a meal, without questioning the waiter regarding the meaning of the mysterious words on the bill of fare.

These Transsylvanian fancy names are often a riddle even to Hungarians, not all of whom are familiar with them. As most of these Transsylvanian dishes—especially the sweets—are prepared with the help of special ingredients and implements on charcoal fires, and therefore unavailable elsewhere, the opportunity to sample them should not be missed.

One of Hungary's most famous specialities is the fish called "Fogas" of Lake Balaton, a delicious fish, which is served in every place, either steamed or grilled. Another delicacy is goose-liver, either roasted or as "pâté de foie gras." This product can be obtained abroad and is sold in almost all first-class food stores in every big city in Europe. Crayfish (in Hungarian, Rák) is a much sought after speciality and is served in soup, in stews and many other ways. In the autumn and winter months there is a great variety of game and wild fowl ; these, however, are also exported to England and many other countries, as well as turkey, pullets, and so on.

Everybody will visit the famous Budapest pastry shops and sample some of the cakes. There is no need to recommend them—they are unsurpassed. The skill of the pastrycooks, combined with the unrivalled quality of the Hungarian flour, results in an endless variety of the finest cakes to be found anywhere. There is no possibility of disappointment in this respect.

It goes without saying that bread and rolls are of the finest quality, and are to be had in great variety, all of them light, crisp, and delicious. Several Hungarian cheese specialities are on sale in England, but it may be mentioned here that the so-called Shepherd Cheese of Hortobágy is served with different ingredients and is mixed at the table according to taste ; besides the cheese, there is butter, caraway seeds, paprika, chopped chive, chopped capers, etc. A little of each, together with a few drops of beer, is mixed with butter and cheese. Of other Hungarian cheeses, the best known are " Magyaróvár," " Pál Puszta," and " Döry." Sweet red pepper fruit, in Hungarian " Paradicsom-paprika," sliced and sprinkled with salt, is eaten with cheese. This raw paprika fruit is sweet, juicy and very healthy.

To finish the meal, the traveller should always order the fruits of the season ; especially peaches, apricots, cherries, all varieties of melon and the muscatel grapes are recommended. Pears and plums are also good.

For the rest, I refer the reader to choose from the dishes described in this book, and, to accompany them, from the wines mentioned in the Appendix.

It is to be hoped that all who enjoyed their holidays in Hungary will agree with the poet

" Ki a Tisza vizét issza,
Vágyik annak szive vissza ! "

(" Whoever drinks of the River Tisza—will be always longing to return ").

HUNGARIAN WINES

Hungary is one of the foremost wine-growing countries in the world. Its climate, its many chains of hills, and its centuries' old tradition in wine-growing and wine-making all contribute to the production of its varied and excellent wines. Hungarian wines possess a spicy bouquet and contain a comparatively low percentage of acids. There is a perfect harmony between the sugar, acid and alcohol content, and most Hungarian wines are of such pleasant taste that they appeal not only to connoisseurs but even to people whose palates are not trained to enjoy wines.

81

At Budafok, near Budapest, the capital of Hungary, there is a wine museum, where about 120 sorts of Hungary's finest wines from the best vintage years are preserved. No traveller to Hungary should fail to visit this museum, which forms part of a special State College, where future experts are trained in the growing, harvesting, handling, making, storing and bottling of wine. Graduates of this college are also in control of all wine leaving the country for export. Wine-growing and wine production is to a large degree under the control of the State, which also owns extensive vineyards and wine cellars. Most Hungarian wines obtainable in Great Britain come from these cellars. All Hungarian wines are natural wines, the law forbidding the addition of sugar, alcohol, etc., to grape wines.

World-famous for centuries are the wines grown and made in the " Tokaj-Hegyalja " district, in the north-east of Hungary, covering about 12,000 acres and about thirty parishes. According to Hungarian law, this is a " closed territory," where no wine grown in other districts may be imported, except with special permission for personal use of the population.

The wine harvest in Tokaj lasts from the end of October until the middle of November, ending with picturesque festivals. The peculiar climate of this district causes the grapes to remain on the stalks until they reach the state of shrunk raisins and in favourable circumstances are just a little frostbitten. On the quantity each season of these shrunk grapes depend the different products of the Tokaj district. If there are enough shrunk berries for the purpose, these are picked separately, placed in tanks on day of picking and a certain quantity of unfermented Tokaj grapejuice is poured over them to dissolve the shrunk grapes. For example, if over two pails of shrunk grapes, each containing 25 quarts of grapes, 34 gallons of unfermented Tokaj grapejuice are poured to dissolve them, the resulting Essence (Aszúbor) is called " 2 pail Essence" (2 puttonyos Aszúbor), and up to " 5 pail Essence " (5 puttonyos Aszúbor) is produced in good vintage years. The number of pails of shrunk grapes used in the making are always marked on the bottles containing Tokaj Essence Wines ; it is therefore useful to know its meaning, when buying this wine, one of the world's finest and rarest. If, however, the amount of shrunk grapes is not sufficient to produce Essence of Tokaj, then all grapes are gathered together, and the so-called " Ordinarium " wine is produced, a very fine white wine. If the harvest of shrunk grapes is especially poor and the standard of good " Ordinarium " cannot be reached, then a wine called " Tokaj Szamorodni " is produced, a very good, but rather dry white wine.

Tokaj Essence or " Aszú " is rich in phosphates of magnesium and of lime, and has remarkable restoring qualities, even when given to patients almost beyond hope of recovery. It is a well-known fact that King Edward VII derived great benefit from this wonderful wine when seized with illness before his Coronation. The wine was sent to him by the Emperor Francis Joseph of Austria-Hungary, from his Imperial cellars.

HUNGARIAN WINE DICTIONARY

BADACSONY. White-wine producing district in the west of Hungary, on the north shores of Lake Balaton. This chain of hills is of volcanic origin. The finest wine produced in this district is "Badacsonyi Szürke Burgundi" or "Auvergnas Gris"; a wine with a pleasant Muscatel flavour grown in this district is "Badacsonyi Muskotály," and another well-known wine is "Badacsonyi Kéknyelü," a very dry white wine.

DEBRÖ. One of the best white wines of Hungary is "Debröi Hárslevelü."

EGER or ERLAU. Red-wine producing district in the north of Hungary. Of the fine, dark blue grapes of this district several excellent red wines are produced, the best known being "Egri Bikavér" or "ox-blood," a heavy Burgundy type of wine; "Egri burgundi" is a light Burgundy type, whereas "Nemes Kadarka" is a lovely wine of Port type.

KECSKEMÉT. White-wine producing district in the south of Hungary. "Kecskeméti Édes Furmint" is of sweet Sauterne type; "Kecskeméti Édes Leányka" is a pleasant, rather heavy, sweet white wine, whereas "Kecskeméti Rizling" is a dry, hock type wine.

PÉCS or FÜNFKIRCHEN. White-wine producing district in the south of Hungary, producing "Pécsi Furmint," of Moselle type.

SOMLÓ. White-wine district, best known by "Somlói Furmint," of Moselle type.

TOKAJ. White-wine producing district in north-east of Hungary, producing the finest Hungarian wines. "Tokaji Aszú" or Essence of Tokaj, ranging from 2 to 5 pail or "puttonyos" varieties, mostly Muscatel flavoured. "Tokaj Ordinarius," a very fine white wine; "Tokaji Szamorodni," a dry, fine white wine.

VILLÁNY. A district near Pécs, producing both red and white wines. "Villányi Vörös" is the red, "Villányi Fehér" the white, and "Villányi Muskotály" a muscatel flavoured, sweet white wine.

INDEX

Velö tojással (Scrambled eggs and brain), 25
Vese gombával (Kidney and mushrooms), 26
Vese velövel (Kidney with brain), 26

STEWS
Bárány pörkölt (Lamb stew, including mutton, pork, veal-stew), 28
Bárány paprikás (Lamb stew, including mutton, pork, veal-stew), 28
Bográcsos csirke (Casserole chicken), 28
Cigány gulyás (Gipsy stew), 29
Kolozsvári káposzta (Transsylvanian pork and cabbage pie), 29
Lucskos káposzta (Transsylvanian-Saxon stew), 30
Magyar gulyás (Hungarian stew), 30
Szegedi Gulyás (Szeged-stew), 30
Székely gulyás (Transsylvanian stew), 31
Tök paprikás (Paprika meat with vegetable marrow), 31

ROASTS, STEAKS
Borjúszelet vadászmódra (Hunters' veal steaks), 33
Eszterházy Rostélyos (Beefsteak à la Eszterházy), 33
Honvéd szelet (Soldiers' steaks), 33
Kolbászos hús (Pork stuffed with sausage), 34
Pesti vesepecsenye (Roast beef of Budapest), 34
Rablóhús or Rablópecsenye (Highwayman's mixed grill), 34
Rakott vesepecsenye (Hungarian hot-pot), 35
Szalonnás sült (Larded steak), 36
Szombathelyi sült (Braised, stuffed beef rolls), 36

POULTRY
Császár jérce (Emperor's pullet), 38
Csirke paprikás (Paprika chicken), 38
Csirke pörkölt (Paprika chicken), 38
Pulyka pörkölt (Turkey stew), 38
Rántott csirke (Fried chicken), 39
Vagdalt libamelle (Minced goosebreast), 39

GAME
Fürj székely módra (Transsylvanian quail), 41
Nyúlpörkölt (Stewed hare), 41
Nyúlpaprikás (Stewed hare), 41
Vaddisznó pörkölt or paprikás (Stewed boar), 41

SAUCES
Áfonya mártás (Cranberry sauce), 42
Ecetes tormamártás (Cold horse radish sauce), 43
Egres mártás (Gooseberry sauce), 43
Metélöhagyma mártás hidegen (Cold chive sauce), 43
Metélöhagyma mártás melegen (Warm chive sauce), 43
Paradicsom mártás (Tomato sauce), 43
Paprika mártás (Paprika sauce), 44

87

A CATALOGUE OF SELECTED DOVER BOOKS
IN ALL FIELDS OF INTEREST

A CATALOGUE OF SELECTED DOVER
BOOKS IN ALL FIELDS OF INTEREST

RACKHAM'S COLOR ILLUSTRATIONS FOR WAGNER'S RING. Rackham's finest mature work—all 64 full-color watercolors in a faithful and lush interpretation of the *Ring*. Full-sized plates on coated stock of the paintings used by opera companies for authentic staging of Wagner. Captions aid in following complete Ring cycle. Introduction. 64 illustrations plus vignettes. 72pp. 8⅝ x 11¼.   23779-6 Pa. $6.00

CONTEMPORARY POLISH POSTERS IN FULL COLOR, edited by Joseph Czestochowski. 46 full-color examples of brilliant school of Polish graphic design, selected from world's first museum (near Warsaw) dedicated to poster art. Posters on circuses, films, plays, concerts all show cosmopolitan influences, free imagination. Introduction. 48pp. 9⅜ x 12¼.
23780-X Pa. $6.00

GRAPHIC WORKS OF EDVARD MUNCH, Edvard Munch. 90 haunting, evocative prints by first major Expressionist artist and one of the greatest graphic artists of his time: *The Scream, Anxiety, Death Chamber, The Kiss, Madonna*, etc. Introduction by Alfred Werner. 90pp. 9 x 12.
23765-6 Pa. $5.00

THE GOLDEN AGE OF THE POSTER, Hayward and Blanche Cirker. 70 extraordinary posters in full colors, from Maitres de l'Affiche, Mucha, Lautrec, Bradley, Cheret, Beardsley, many others. Total of 78pp. 9⅜ x 12¼.   22753-7 Pa. $5.95

THE NOTEBOOKS OF LEONARDO DA VINCI, edited by J. P. Richter. Extracts from manuscripts reveal great genius; on painting, sculpture, anatomy, sciences, geography, etc. Both Italian and English. 186 ms. pages reproduced, plus 500 additional drawings, including studies for *Last Supper*, Sforza monument, etc. 860pp. 7⅞ x 10¾. (Available in U.S. only)
22572-0, 22573-9 Pa., Two-vol. set $15.90

THE CODEX NUTTALL, as first edited by Zelia Nuttall. Only inexpensive edition, in full color, of a pre-Columbian Mexican (Mixtec) book. 88 color plates show kings, gods, heroes, temples, sacrifices. New explanatory, historical introduction by Arthur G. Miller. 96pp. 11⅜ x 8½. (Available in U.S. only)   23168-2 Pa. $7.95

UNE SEMAINE DE BONTÉ, A SURREALISTIC NOVEL IN COLLAGE, Max Ernst. Masterpiece created out of 19th-century periodical illustrations, explores worlds of terror and surprise. Some consider this Ernst's greatest work. 208pp. 8⅛ x 11.   23252-2 Pa. $6.00

THE AMERICAN SENATOR, Anthony Trollope. Little known, long unavailable Trollope novel on a grand scale. Here are humorous comment on American vs. English culture, and stunning portrayal of a heroine/villainess. Superb evocation of Victorian village life. 561pp. 5⅜ x 8½.
23801-6 Pa. $6.00

WAS IT MURDER? James Hilton. The author of *Lost Horizon* and *Goodbye, Mr. Chips* wrote one detective novel (under a pen-name) which was quickly forgotten and virtually lost, even at the height of Hilton's fame. This edition brings it back—a finely crafted public school puzzle resplendent with Hilton's stylish atmosphere. A thoroughly English thriller by the creator of Shangri-la. 252pp. 5⅜ x 8. (Available in U.S. only)
23774-5 Pa. $3.00

CENTRAL PARK: A PHOTOGRAPHIC GUIDE, Victor Laredo and Henry Hope Reed. 121 superb photographs show dramatic views of Central Park: Bethesda Fountain, Cleopatra's Needle, Sheep Meadow, the Blockhouse, plus people engaged in many park activities: ice skating, bike riding, etc. Captions by former Curator of Central Park, Henry Hope Reed, provide historical view, changes, etc. Also photos of N.Y. landmarks on park's periphery. 96pp. 8½ x 11. 23750-8 Pa. $4.50

NANTUCKET IN THE NINETEENTH CENTURY, Clay Lancaster. 180 rare photographs, stereographs, maps, drawings and floor plans recreate unique American island society. Authentic scenes of shipwreck, lighthouses, streets, homes are arranged in geographic sequence to provide walking-tour guide to old Nantucket existing today. Introduction, captions. 160pp. 8⅞ x 11¾. 23747-8 Pa. $6.95

STONE AND MAN: A PHOTOGRAPHIC EXPLORATION, Andreas Feininger. 106 photographs by *Life* photographer Feininger portray man's deep passion for stone through the ages. Stonehenge-like megaliths, fortified towns, sculpted marble and crumbling tenements show textures, beauties, fascination. 128pp. 9¼ x 10¾. 23756-7 Pa. $5.95

CIRCLES, A MATHEMATICAL VIEW, D. Pedoe. Fundamental aspects of college geometry, non-Euclidean geometry, and other branches of mathematics: representing circle by point. Poincare model, isoperimetric property, etc. Stimulating recreational reading. 66 figures. 96pp. 5⅝ x 8¼.
63698-4 Pa. $2.75

THE DISCOVERY OF NEPTUNE, Morton Grosser. Dramatic scientific history of the investigations leading up to the actual discovery of the eighth planet of our solar system. Lucid, well-researched book by well-known historian of science. 172pp. 5⅜ x 8½. 23726-5 Pa. $3.50

THE DEVIL'S DICTIONARY. Ambrose Bierce. Barbed, bitter, brilliant witticisms in the form of a dictionary. Best, most ferocious satire America has produced. 145pp. 5⅜ x 8½. 20487-1 Pa. $2.25

THE CURVES OF LIFE, Theodore A. Cook. Examination of shells, leaves, horns, human body, art, etc., in *"the* classic reference on how the golden ratio applies to spirals and helices in nature . . . . "—Martin Gardner. 426 illustrations. Total of 512pp. 5⅜ x 8½. 23701-X Pa. $5.95

AN ILLUSTRATED FLORA OF THE NORTHERN UNITED STATES AND CANADA, Nathaniel L. Britton, Addison Brown. Encyclopedic work covers 4666 species, ferns on up. Everything. Full botanical information, illustration for each. This earlier edition is preferred by many to more recent revisions. 1913 edition. Over 4000 illustrations, total of 2087pp. 6⅛ x 9¼. 22642-5, 22643-3, 22644-1 Pa., Three-vol. set $25.50

MANUAL OF THE GRASSES OF THE UNITED STATES, A. S. Hitchcock, U.S. Dept. of Agriculture. The basic study of American grasses, both indigenous and escapes, cultivated and wild. Over 1400 species. Full descriptions, information. Over 1100 maps, illustrations. Total of 1051pp. 5⅜ x 8½. 22717-0, 22718-9 Pa., Two-vol. set $15.00

THE CACTACEAE,, Nathaniel L. Britton, John N. Rose. Exhaustive, definitive. Every cactus in the world. Full botanical descriptions. Thorough statement of nomenclatures, habitat, detailed finding keys. The one book needed by every cactus enthusiast. Over 1275 illustrations. Total of 1080pp. 8 x 10¼. 21191-6, 21192-4 Clothbd., Two-vol. set $35.00

AMERICAN MEDICINAL PLANTS, Charles F. Millspaugh. Full descriptions, 180 plants covered: history; physical description; methods of preparation with all chemical constituents extracted; all claimed curative or adverse effects. 180 full-page plates. Classification table. 804pp. 6½ x 9¼. 23034-1 Pa. $12.95

A MODERN HERBAL, Margaret Grieve. Much the fullest, most exact, most useful compilation of herbal material. Gigantic alphabetical encyclopedia, from aconite to zedoary, gives botanical information, medical properties, folklore, economic uses, and much else. Indispensable to serious reader. 161 illustrations. 888pp. 6½ x 9¼. (Available in U.S. only) 22798-7, 22799-5 Pa., Two-vol. set $13.00

THE HERBAL or GENERAL HISTORY OF PLANTS, John Gerard. The 1633 edition revised and enlarged by Thomas Johnson. Containing almost 2850 plant descriptions and 2705 superb illustrations, Gerard's *Herbal* is a monumental work, the book all modern English herbals are derived from, the one herbal every serious enthusiast should have in its entirety. Original editions are worth perhaps $750. 1678pp. 8½ x 12¼. 23147-X Clothbd. $50.00

MANUAL OF THE TREES OF NORTH AMERICA, Charles S. Sargent. The basic survey of every native tree and tree-like shrub, 717 species in all. Extremely full descriptions, information on habitat, growth, locales, economics, etc. Necessary to every serious tree lover. Over 100 finding keys. 783 illustrations. Total of 986pp. 5⅜ x 8½. 20277-1, 20278-X Pa., Two-vol. set $11.00

GEOMETRY, RELATIVITY AND THE FOURTH DIMENSION, Rudolf Rucker. Exposition of fourth dimension, means of visualization, concepts of relativity as Flatland characters continue adventures. Popular, easily followed yet accurate, profound. 141 illustrations. 133pp. 5⅜ x 8½.
23400-2 Pa. $2.75

THE ORIGIN OF LIFE, A. I. Oparin. Modern classic in biochemistry, the first rigorous examination of possible evolution of life from nitrocarbon compounds. Non-technical, easily followed. Total of 295pp. 5⅜ x 8½.
60213-3 Pa. $4.00

PLANETS, STARS AND GALAXIES, A. E. Fanning. Comprehensive introductory survey: the sun, solar system, stars, galaxies, universe, cosmology; quasars, radio stars, etc. 24pp. of photographs. 189pp. 5⅜ x 8½. (Available in U.S. only)
21680-2 Pa. $3.75

THE THIRTEEN BOOKS OF EUCLID'S ELEMENTS, translated with introduction and commentary by Sir Thomas L. Heath. Definitive edition. Textual and linguistic notes, mathematical analysis, 2500 years of critical commentary. Do not confuse with abridged school editions. Total of 1414pp. 5⅜ x 8½.
60088-2, 60089-0, 60090-4 Pa., Three-vol. set $18.50

Prices subject to change without notice.

Available at your book dealer or write for free catalogue to Dept. GI, Dover Publications, Inc., 180 Varick St., N.Y., N.Y. 10014. Dover publishes more than 175 books each year on science, elementary and advanced mathematics, biology, music, art, literary history, social sciences and other areas.